Raw, Naked & Fearless

11 Principles For Living Your Greatest Life!

Ricardo Cruz Leal

This book is dedicated to you!
The 'you' that is seeking more.

Ricardo Cruz Leal

CONTENTS

"The greatest achievement of a human being is to one day realize that they are and always have been connected to a universal soul, that they are more powerful and more capable than they have ever imagined, that they are not insignificant evolutionary happenings but instead the architects of their entire worldly experience!"

—**Ricardo Cruz Leal**

Ricardo Cruz Leal

.

INTRODUCTION

What if reading this book could actually change your life? What if you knew with absolute certainty, and with the same conviction that you have in knowing that the morning sun will eventually rise, that by reading the words on these pages you would awaken a dormant power sleeping inside you right now that would allow you to not only have the things you have always wanted, but to become the person that you have always wanted to be? What if all you had to do was to learn these principles, apply them, and then magic would start to happen?

Would you do it?

Would you invest the time now, so that in the near future you could just be you and have the kind of life you have always dreamt of, free of stress and heavy burdens, connected and truly alive? Or would you pass, claiming that you don't have time, don't believe, or don't care?

Whatever you decide, the truth is that something led you to this book and to this opportunity for change. Maybe you have been actively seeking out ways to improve your life for some time now — reading books, attending seminars, watching videos — or maybe it might just have been a passing thought which normally you would have ignored because, in your mind, you have accepted the current state of affairs and are too frightened to take a chance on greatness. It could also be that you are looking for greater purpose, greater joy, and excitement out of life, and perhaps you have felt like something has been missing for quite some time now. It might be that you feel like you're stuck in a rut and can't seem to climb your way out of it no matter how much willpower you have. Or perhaps your personal struggle with your own image, be it body image or other insecurities, are filling you with anxiety and fear. It may even be that you have tried so hard to become financially free that each time you attempt something new, you lose more money than when you first began. Or maybe you just feel lost and are fucking tired of it!

The reasons for seeking a greater life are endless, and each individual has faced unique challenges throughout their lives. I don't presume to know what yours may be, however, the fact that you have this book in your hands means that you are part of a small minority of human beings that are actually taking back control of their lives. The hardest step, and one that cannot be successfully forced upon anyone, is this initial desire to be and have more! More fun, more love, more resources, more money, more excitement, more travel, more health, more life! Unlike the masses, you are not willing to go quietly into the night, and realise that your precious time on this earth is limited and you will not live by default. So by searching for ways to make this happen, you have started the ball rolling, and the more you follow this search, the bigger that ball will become, gaining powerful momentum each time you move forward until it is an unstoppable force that moulds life to your every demand!

The Principles within this book are much more than self-help advice, or law of attraction secrets, they are a manifesto for unleashing your true human potential. They are not typical motivational tools, in fact, not one principle is about motivation. To be honest, this entire manifesto is unlike anything you have ever read before. Willpower is bullshit, goals are counterproductive, grinding is pointless — these are just some of the beliefs that have been programmed into your way of life, a way of life that should be effortless, purposeful, and always flowing naturally. This manifesto will turn your world upside down and allow you to see for the first time that you have not been in control, that your life has been designed by default.

You see, when you discover who and what you are and what you are actually capable of, life will change! You will no longer gossip about people, or worry about the opinions of others. You won't be stressed or anxious about life and all its marvels, you won't feel insecure or threatened. You will, for the first time, be in complete alignment with your true self, and have the epiphany that who you may have thought you wanted to be is not the person you will choose to become.

When you tear away the masks you wear and strip yourself of this fear-based ego you begin to make decisions based on the knowledge that we humans are all connected somehow, that your actions and thoughts truly do affect the universe around you. You will naturally become a compassionate, kind, loving Whole Being, living a life that most people will not understand and may even envy. And that is okay, because as I mentioned before, this is a path that must be sought out and cannot be taught to those who do not seek it. You will find that negative words like envy, jealousy, shame, pity, and entitlement will no longer exist in your vocabulary, and you will come to some powerful realizations that will free you from the hold that your previous programming has had on you. One is that you will feel real happiness when someone else is able to succeed in their life, no matter how they measure their success. Encouragement and positivity is the only angle you will have, and you will no longer be consumed by the need to 'keep up' or 'be better.' Friends, family, and anyone else who happens to come in contact with you will feel that there is something uniquely different about you. They won't be able to put their finger on it, but will realise how your way of being, and the life changes that have occurred, are impressive and it will frustrate the shit out of them as they won't understand how you've done it. They may ask why you are so different, yet you will no longer have the need to advertise your accomplishments but instead will just say something like this: "I'm just in a really good place."

Now they will definitely think you have gone bonkers, and maybe they're right, maybe you just might be crazy, and I can tell you that if you follow this path you will definitely be thought of as crazy by those who can't see the forest through the trees. The ironic part is that the only ones who are truly crazy are the ones who think that living a life on terms other than their own is the 'correct' way to live. Once you give up the bullshit and awaken to your true capabilities you will become an outlier, and naturally move away from anything and anyone that no longer serves your way of being. You may find that hard to believe or even consider but you won't have to move away, they will begin to distance themselves from you on their own.

You will be able to see it happening, as it usually follows a predetermined type of pattern. First, you will be mocked for daring to even think that you could live life on your terms. Then you will be envied because others will notice that you have it all, that life seems to deliver to you all that you want. Finally, they will want to be like you, and will begin asking you how you did it!

So back to the original question — What if this is the book to make it happen?

It could be! I can tell you that this book was not something created out of thin air, and the principles are not just more textbook regurgitation by someone who wants to sell you something. No, these principles were carefully created by years of experience and practice, and are the exact ones that I used to completely change who I was and create a life that at one point seemed unattainable and unrealistic — yet here I am. But I'm not going to tell you my story just yet, I don't want you to think that your life has to be as bad as mine was in order to use these principles. They are the foundation of all human behaviour and apply to any and all possible circumstances, so rest assured that whatever you want to achieve, no matter how simple or how complicated you may think it is, the principles will be your guide.

As I mentioned before, each and every person who has picked up this book, whether they made it past the front cover or are still reading these words right now, has consciously begun to seek a greater life. That is the only pre-requisite to discovering your true capabilities, and unlike those who would mock this book or, like a horse with blinders, be completely oblivious to the possibility that a better life is available, you are already on the right path to living your greatest life. How far you go, and whether this book and these principles ignite your soul remains to be seen. I can't promise you that you will be fully awake, but I can promise you that it will change your life, and maybe it may even transform it! My hope is that by the end of this manifesto you will know who you are and what you are capable of, that you will join me and become a Raw, Naked & Fearless Whole Being!

PRINCIPLE 1

UNDERSTANDING THE MIND

"You are shaped by your thoughts, you become what you think!"

To be able to create a purposeful life and get everything that you consciously desire — be it millions in the bank, everlasting happiness and fulfillment, or inherent vibrancy and health — then you must first understand this fundamental principle. It is, without a doubt, the first order of business and the foundation for everything that you will learn from this manifesto. Without this knowledge, this understanding, your pursuit of an extraordinary life will face seemingly insurmountable challenges. This is why so many before you, who have invested their hard-earned money on self-development resources, have found themselves unable to reach their full potential. Like how dough without yeast fails to rise, missing this one ingredient will likely prevent you from living the life of your dreams. This is the first principle, the principle for which all human life is based on — whether you agree with it or not, is the ultimate truth.

You are your thoughts.

This truth is irrefutable, and once you realise its absoluteness you will be ready to move forward and begin sculpting the life you desire. Understanding this truth will also allow you to see that your current situation in life is a precise and inevitable occurrence that was shaped by each thought that you have ever had, whether it was conscious or otherwise. You are exactly where you should be and, with the precision of a mathematical equation, I will demonstrate this to you. Realizing that a person's life is a result of their thoughts will also help you to see why all humans, all cultures, all races, are exactly the way that they are. This knowing will allow you to open your mind and discover a power that has been used against you up until now — used, without your knowledge, to create the human being you are today. You are living a default life!

Let's dive into this a little deeper, so that you can begin to understand this principle and then use it to examine your own life. I am going to tell you a story about a man I know named John. Once you have read the story, I want you to see if you can compare John's experience to someone in your own life — be it an acquaintance or someone very close to you — and, with an open mind, begin to see the direct relationship between how their thinking has shaped their life experience.

John was always down-on-his-luck. As a matter of fact, most people he knew had a nickname for him — Bad Luck John. John was very aware of his nickname and because bad luck seemed to be a constant in his life, he was never really bothered by it. In fact, he identified strongly with the moniker and could never remember having any good luck at all. Whenever John met up with his friends, he would always be in an uproar about another spout of bad luck he just had. One day it was having his car towed from a parkade, on another he spilled his coffee on himself, he got his wallet stolen at the gym, found out his girlfriend cheated on him, dropped his phone in a puddle, and then once a bird pooped on his head seconds after he looked up and noticed a flock flying by. This was John's life — one bad luck moment after another. From the outside, it really did seem that John was cursed, and no one could seem to remember a time when he got a break. John had a bad job, a bad car, a bad bank balance, and a bad life — and John couldn't understand why!

I'm sure you know somebody in your life right now who has a similar story to John and they too have the exact same issue John had — their life is the precise result of their thoughts! Even if, in their heart of hearts, they wanted to be better and luckier, their current way of thinking would never allow them to change. They have been hardwired for failure.
But how does this happen? If we could examine John's programming, that

makes him think the way he does, from the day he came into this world to the present, from the words of the people around him to the programs he watched on TV, we would see how he created his values, beliefs, and ultimately his life. If we could lay it all out on a board in front of us, our conclusion would be that John is exactly where he should be. We can safely assume that John was unaware of what was happening — in fact, he was sure that he never chose this! He was simply stuck, living a default life based on the programming he had received from a young age and the resulting thoughts that were a direct result of that programming.

Now, let's look at another example.

Joanne has everything going for her. She is the president of a multi-national corporation and is considered an influencer in her industry. She is regularly invited to speak at seminars and has established herself as a leader in her chosen field. Joanne seems to go from good to great in everything she commits to, and her friends have a catchphrase they use for her — 'Joanne just does it'. And it's true, Joanne is always doing it! Whenever she visits her friends they are always excited to hear about the new things she's doing, and she always comes ready with new stories — she met with the president, ran a marathon for charity, won $1,000 on a lottery ticket, bought a new car for the summer, and has decided to travel to Tibet! From the outside, it always looked like Joanne was driven and relentless in her pursuit of excellence, and even she knew that she could pretty much accomplish anything she put her mind to. She had a great car, a great house, a great job, and she couldn't understand why others didn't.

Like with John, I'm sure you have someone in your life that is living a 'Joanne just does it' kind of life. And again, like with John, Joanne is unaware of how she was gifted this type of drive. If we were to look back on Joanne's life, we would be able to see the programming she received from an early age and how it turned into beliefs, values, and memories that created a thinking mind that resulted in exactly what she is today. The fact that one life is culturally accepted as 'better' than the other is irrelevant at this point, what is relevant is that they are both inevitable products of their thinking which was programmed in them by default. Joanne's life is better because her programming was better; hence her thinking is better; hence her life seems better. For the sake of this explanation I am not going to get into a discussion about the other areas of their life — maybe Joanne feels miserable all the time despite her success and maybe John is a great human being. Those factors would be a result of their programming and thinking as well, and dissecting their whole lives would give us their exact nature, but we don't need to discuss every variable to get to the point.

All you need to know is that **all of who you are** right now, is exactly who you should be!

Let that sink in and settle for a while.

It's a daunting thought that you are exactly where you should be, especially if where you are is not where you want to be. I know that self-reflection can be difficult, but if you allow yourself to really think about the specific programming that you received, you will come to the realization that the thoughts that you have, the mind that you live with, the life that you have, is, in fact, the one you should have. This will lead you into retrospection and will make you visit times, people, and places throughout your life that might bring up some pretty bad feelings, maybe even anger. You might start blaming your parents, your circumstances, your friends, your teachers for the type of mind that you currently have and the kind of life you unwittingly created. Once you are able to move past blaming others — which is a belief that comes from programming itself — you can observe your own history from a third person point-of-view. Look back through your life as if you are floating above, seeing yourself experiencing your past. Be the unattached observer to your own life history. Once you view your life as an observer, you will clearly see why you believe the things you do today, and why your life is what it is. This is not about blame, it is the reality of all human minds, and your history, your programming, will soon become your greatest ally in creating new thinking and shaping a new mind to create the life you desire. At this moment, however, the only thing you need to understand is that all the Information you've received throughout your life, especially in your younger years, created your values, beliefs, and memories, which created internal representations in your mind leading to your behaviour. This acts as a feedback loop, because your internal representations also lead to emotions which in turn reinforce the values and beliefs and… you get the picture! It makes change very difficult for the average, unaware person. As you can see from the diagram below, behaviour is the last thing to occur in this flow, and has already been 'pre-determined', shall we say, by all the other facets of the mind. So when someone tries to change a behaviour, they are fighting a losing battle unless they change the other, more influential, areas first.

So, let's review where we are at this point, and expand on this fundamental first principle, the first foundational pillar to achieving *anything* you want. We can now say that your life is a direct and inevitable reflection of your mind. Your mind is comprised of two areas of awareness — a conscious mind and an unconscious mind — which receive all external inputs into a programming filter that includes values, beliefs, and memories. This then creates internal representations such as thoughts and feelings. These internal representations are fed back into your programming filter through your emotions and your subconscious reinforcing the programming. The subconscious mind then overrides any direct conscious will, and delivers the behaviour externally as is internally mandated. Your mind and body are a direct reflection of this internal process.

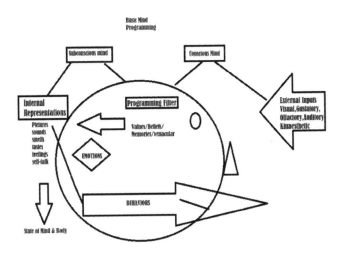

Most people have a general understanding of what the mind is, but usually only the basics from diagrams and material learned in the human anatomy section of biology class — if you even took biology that is! Nevertheless, I am not here to discuss the biological breakdown of the human mind, all we are interested in is how it ultimately functions when it comes to our subjective life experience, and how it receives, stores, and processes information into real behaviour, and real results. I am not interested in the firing of neurons and the dividing of the Cerebrum into quantifiable parts. In fact, what I propose here goes far beyond the physical material of the brain, and into the unquantifiable and powerful 'being' that we are! My goal is to give you this knowledge, this fundamental truth that will allow you to apply all the other principles in this manifesto to create a life you never thought possible.

All of our programming is received via our five senses and comes into our mind via two areas called the subconscious and the conscious mind. Although there is more here to learn, we will be focusing on these two widely recognized aspects of the mind, so that you will have a solid foundation before we go down the rabbit hole and uncover other areas of the mind that are hidden from us, both figuratively and literally.

Firstly, let's discuss the subconscious mind and identify what it does and what it is. Your subconscious mind is the regulator. It is the part of your brain that generates and maintains habits, and delivers whatever instructions it has been programmed to deliver. It does not care what the input is, and will ensure that you behave in the manner that fulfills its instructions. Whether you intentionally created these instructions or not, it will always remain faithful to your programming regardless of what your conscious mind tells it.

Let's look at overeating as an example. People who struggle with their weight because of eating too much have memories and beliefs that have been programmed, usually during their childhood, into internal representations. Someone who cannot control their eating habits might think of food and immediately trigger memories and beliefs that caused them to eat to avoid pain or suffering, which in turn forms an internal representation of gratification, comfort, and acceptance. These are powerful emotions that are directly related to food. The subconscious takes this information and turns it into behaviour that results in overeating to feel gratified and comforted. No matter how many times this person consciously says, 'I will not overeat', their subconscious will ultimately override that thought and they will end up eating too much. The subconscious is simply doing what it was told — protecting them from unwanted feelings.

The problem is that old instructions like this, old programming, is not serving you anymore and, in fact, is probably keeping you from being the best you can be. The subconscious is the greatest servant, yet it is also the cruellest master!

Now, let's take a look at the conscious mind. This is your active mind, the one that invokes action. It's the part of your brain that causes you to raise your hand when you think about raising your hand or hit the brakes when you see a red light. The best way to describe it, without getting into complex jargon and explanations, is that this is your 'NOW' mind. It acts only in the now — 'now I'm going to get a drink of water' or 'now I'm going to change the channel'. You can look at this mind as the actor, it acts upon your 'NOW' life. The irony is that once you have enough 'now' moments, those moments or instructions get locked in and behaviour begins to form. This moulding of conscious thought into behaviour is also being registered by your subconscious mind — it's picking up all the underlying feelings and emotions attached to every 'now' moment. So, in essence, whatever you consciously think will eventually affect the subconscious, especially if those thoughts are believable, emotional, and repetitive.

To recap, the sum of all the conscious 'NOW' thoughts in your life have created programming filters that have been reinforced by your emotions forming powerful internal representations. These internal representations are regulated by the subconscious, and will deliver behaviour in line with its programming. So, all that you really consciously control are the 'now' decisions in your everyday life. You are consciously choosing to read this right now, yet the way you feel about it, or how you perceive the information and whether you align with it or not is happening subconsciously and is being decided based on the sum total of all the previous experiences you have had in relation to this subject matter.

To make this a little easier to understand I have created a flow chart called the *Behaviour Mind Loop*. This helps you to identify any behavioural patterns that you currently have and realise why you get the results that you get based on these behaviours.

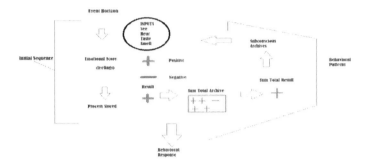

Once an event, or behaviour, has generated a result, that event is archived in your subconscious mind and will influence your behaviour from that point forward. The more the result is strengthened, the more the subconscious influences the behaviour. This will create patterns and default behaviours regardless of the conscious effort made to try and change that behaviour.

So what does it take to achieve greatness, or wake up feeling energized and excited every single morning? What does it take to see and act on opportunities that bring you financial freedom? What does it take to be an entrepreneur, or an engineer? The truth is that there are very predictable patterns in achieving a specific result in life. A person who is financially free has a very specific way of thinking, this thinking was created through the sum total of his or her experiences and results in a very specific type of behaviour that delivers money. It is really that simple!
There have been hundreds of books written about how to replicate the behaviours and actions of successful people — *The 7 Habits of Highly Effective People*, *The 9 Steps to Financial Freedom*, *Think and Grow Rich*, *How to Win Friends and Influence People* — and the list goes on. These are all wonderfully powerful and insightful books, however, just because you learn what someone else has learned doesn't mean you will achieve what they did. Why not? The programming in their minds is very different from yours and, without addressing that programming, there is no way to effectively get the same results. It is why most programs or systems always have a little

disclaimer that says, 'results are not typical', because you can't teach someone a new way of thinking without first teaching them how to review their subconscious programming and then change and mould it to get the desired results. This whole book is designed to give you that power — the power to actively change your programming, to free yourself from limiting behaviours and thoughts, and to create your life on purpose.

By now you will have realised that your behaviours, and the behaviours of the people around you, are exactly what they should be based on your programming. And, although it might be hard to swallow especially if you think you have had a hard life and were less fortunate than others around you, you now know that it was the programming that you allowed in and/or gave to your mind that brought you to where you are today. You also know that the friends you have, the city you live in, the country you are a citizen of, also have a certain way of behaving in accordance to the education system, the television programs you watch, and the overall programming of the general populace. You can see that even the overall beliefs and values of a culture are just programmed behaviour. This is why people use the phrase 'you are the company you keep', yet they have never really contemplated the power and the effect that this has on entire societies. The beauty of this knowledge is that you can now be aware of the fact that you are not just 'you' by mistake, you are, in a sense, a 'manufactured' you! The person you think you are is exactly that, an assortment of thoughts based on values and beliefs that have been programmed into your mind via the senses, and reinforced through emotion and repetition. Knowing this, and contemplating the power it holds over you, should immediately make you want to reassess everything and anything you've allowed to permeate your mind!

This foundational pillar of knowledge has been used to manipulate you throughout your life for a variety of reasons. We can look at one right now (when you do the *Master Training* at the end of this chapter, you will have the opportunity to think about how many others there are). Now, I want you to picture Santa Clause. What colour is his suit? Red, right? Almost everyone on the planet will agree with you, but the real question is, why? Not why it's red, but why does everyone seem to know this answer? If you have been paying attention you will now know that the reason for the mass acceptance of Santa wearing red is because you were programmed from an early age to believe and accept it. It is rooted in our culture. What you didn't know, or probably never wondered, is why does Santa wear a red suit? How did it all begin? Who or what gave us these thoughts? Was it your parents, your teachers, TV, advertising, movies? If yes, where did they get the idea from? The truth is that Santa's 'Red Suit' was created by the Coca-Cola company! It's true! This beverage company, known around the world, created it for an advertising campaign years ago, and programmed generations into associating the colour red with Santa, and with Coke!

Your mind is not your own! The rawest, most genuine **you** lies beyond your programmed beliefs which have created a life that you are not in control of. It's time to take back your mind and discover the incredible power which has always been within you, a raw power waiting to be unleashed. A power that will awaken your true capabilities and allow you to transform any aspect of your life.

Master Training

A Master Training section will be found at the end of each chapter and gives you an opportunity to apply what you have learned so far.

I encourage you to write your thoughts down in the space below, or grab a notebook and write your answers down so that you can begin working through your programming and transforming your life!

- What is an example of a strong belief that you hold?

- When that belief is challenged, how does it make you feel?

- Can you look back and see who and what instilled that belief in you?

- What things/events/people reinforce your belief?

- Do you tend to dismiss ideas that oppose your belief?

- How does this belief affect your behavior?

- If you didn't have this belief how would things look to you?

- What internal representations do you have about your belief?

- What memories do you have about this belief?

- If your life experience was different, can you see that you would have a completely different belief, and therefore different behavior?

- What is an example of a cultural belief that you hold?

- How difficult would it be to change a belief that is culturally ingrained and has created a deep internal representation inside your mind?

- What beliefs do you have that are preventing you from living a life of abundance and happiness?

- How did you form those internal representations?

PRINCIPLE 2

SELF-AWARENESS — WHAT AM I DOING?

In the first chapter, you learned how your mind works and were able to understand — maybe even for the first time — why it is that you are living the kind of life you are living. That first step, that foundational pillar, that knowledge that you now have, naturally leads us to the next principle — becoming a master at being aware of the programming that you have within! You are going to learn about 'self-awareness' and by the end of this step, you will be able to actively observe your thoughts, behaviours, and patterns and understand how they are constantly shaping your reality. Once you become more self-aware, you take back the power to choose what thoughts you focus on and ultimately learn how you create your life on purpose.

At this point, you might be thinking 'what the hell is this guy talking about?!', which is totally fair. In fact, I'm thinking the same thing — except, unlike most people, I think about it *all the time*, automatically, by default. I am always consciously thinking about what the hell it is that I'm thinking.

Did I lose you there? Let me explain.

I have made my self-awareness automatic, so that I am always in a state of self-awareness. I am always monitoring my own thoughts at any given moment because I have spent years practicing, testing, and mastering it. Don't worry though! It won't take you that long to master self-awareness

—I'm going to give you all the tools and shortcuts that I've learned so that you can benefit from this amazing 'hidden knowledge' in the least amount of time possible.

What's hidden knowledge?

It's no secret that you can be aware of your own thoughts. Think about phrases you've said, or heard others say, like: "I've got a little angel on one shoulder and a little devil on the other", "I'm just talking to myself", or "the little voice inside my head is telling me….". You get the picture. On some level, we understand that there is a dialogue going on in our heads. We have always known it, yet we were never taught how to decipher it, to understand it, to use it! I wish that our education system had taught me this knowledge as a child, it would have had such an impact on my life and saved me from having to discover it alone. (It is because of this that one of my goals in life is to have as many young people read this manifesto and learn the *Eleven Principles* before they encounter the roadblocks and pitfalls of life.)

The first thing we need to do is pinpoint exactly what it is we want to be 'aware' of. I want you to commit to following the techniques at the end of this chapter and really embrace what will be one of the greatest tools I will share with you in this manifesto. First, I need you to read the following statement of intent, out loud, as many times as it takes for you to believe it and mean it:

"I commit to mastering the art of self-awareness by using the tools I have been given, and the more I read these words, the more I realise that I have already begun to understand the power it will give me, and the more power I get, the easier it will become to be aware, and the more aware I become the more my life begins to change, and the more my life changes the more I get what I have always wanted."

The next step is consciously finding the 'voice' that you want to be aware of. But, before we continue let's identify what this 'voice' is not, so that by process of elimination we can discover the 'other voice' or 'subconscious chatter' that we want to hone in on.

It is important to understand that this voice is not your directed thoughts — it is not the willful thoughts you use to direct your mind and your actions. For example, If I decide that I am going to pause writing to get myself a coffee, my legs take hold of my body and I begin standing and moving in the direction of the kitchen. Those thoughts, that direction, is a Conscious Thought Process, a CTP. CTPs drive what we call our 'free will' and are the part of thinking that we do that drives action and that we can easily control. The tricky part is that usually those CTPs are formed by previous thoughts that were subconscious in nature, and are also followed by thoughts that are subconscious in nature. These pre- and post-CTP thoughts are called the Subconscious Thought Process, or STP. Sometimes you have a 'free will' CTP, but usually your CTP is the result of an STP, and then is followed by more STPs. So, in reality, there are very few isolated CTPs and, therefore, you really don't have as many moments of 'free will' as you may think.

Let me simplify this with an equation.

Free will or spontaneous action = CTP (Conscious Thought Process)

Subconscious influence pre- and post-CTP = STP (Subconscious Thought Process)

Having more CTPs than STPs is what is known as 'Zen'. Being in a state of Zen means that you are living life one spontaneous moment after another, unaffected by thought. It's pure living, pure free will, and is what Zen masters achieve, or attempt to achieve, throughout their life. Well achieving Zen is a remarkable way to live, we are not going to go quite that far. My goal is to give you the knowledge and tools to use this ancient art of enlightenment to affect your life in magnificent ways, developing the power to direct your life in ways you never thought possible.

So, let's take a closer look at CTPs so that we can understand the relationship they have with STPs. The easiest way to know what a CTP is, is to understand the words you use in your thoughts. As I mentioned earlier, you have very few pure CTPs and most of your day is comprised of STPs. In fact, only about 5% of your daily thoughts are actually free will thoughts (CTPs).

What language or words would a CTP consist of?

Firstly, they would be void of any emotional words such as 'love', 'hate', 'angry', or 'frustrated', and would be primarily action based. For example: 'I am going to go to the bathroom', 'I am standing up', 'I am going to walk up the stairs', 'I am reading'. They are very simple, very direct, action-based thoughts. If you add in a feeling or reason they are no longer CTPs, or free will thoughts. Instead, they are thoughts that are subconscious in nature and as a result have influenced your behaviour. If we take one of the above statements and add a feeling to it, we can begin to understand how CTPs are influenced by STPs. For example, 'I am going to walk up the stairs to get away from your nagging', is no longer a free will thought. You might think it is, that you've decided to go up the stairs because you were getting annoyed, but actually, your previous programming that resulted in you feeling annoyed is what drove the thought. Let's look at another example. If you were to say: 'I am going to read to become a better me', you can begin to see that the driving force to read came from the programming in your subconscious that makes you want to be better and makes you believe that reading will make you better. Understanding this concept, and becoming aware of this relationship between your thoughts, will make you a very powerful and unique individual, unlike the majority of people living default lives — this is freedom, my friend.

Now that we know what an STP does, and how it makes us believe that our decisions are 'free will' even if they aren't, this leads us to realise that in order to make true change we need to monitor and manipulate these STPs in our favor so that we can actually create what we want in life. In order to do this, we need to become aware of the STPs as they occur, and use the right thinking, the right words, to drive the desired behaviour . This is the awareness I want to give you, so that eventually you can instantly adapt your thinking and always make decisions based on your 'conscious goals', which will make them easily attainable, without having to employ willpower or gain added stress!

It is easier now to look back at past events with clarity and see how this process created every behaviour and reaction you've had throughout your life. But, although this is a powerful insight, it does nothing for real-time events. What it does do, however, is give you the knowledge and ability to develop a sense of awareness that will allow you to almost instantaneously re-align the subconscious thoughts on the fly, choosing which ones to accept, ignore, or alter to your benefit. So, for now, we will continue down the rabbit hole by learning how to listen to those STPs, and later in this manifesto you will learn the right techniques to use in order to get the desired results. Right now, I want you to become a master at just consciously listening to the subconscious chatter so that later you will be able to make it your servant and dramatically improve your life.

I want you to think about a specific time when the subconscious chatter was happening without your awareness, or at least without your focused attention. Remember a time when you were driving, maybe it was earlier today, or yesterday, or maybe a specific drive you took that just happened to pop into your mind and you found yourself arriving at a certain point and had the thought 'wow, I don't even remember the last few minutes of driving'. Go back to that instance now and think about how you practically drove on autopilot, lost in your own thoughts, hypnotized by the routine of the driving experience. This is the perfect example of a time when your mind, your subconscious mind, was running with thoughts that you were not consciously directing, they were flowing without your active involvement. These thoughts are STPs, and are part of the subconscious programming you learned about in the first principle. Although you may have started with a direct thought, your mind quickly took over, and you probably lost track of exactly what it was that you were thinking. Another great example is what happens during your morning shower. Here too, you are often in a trance where your subconscious mind is running away with your thoughts, directing your affairs without your active involvement. It is these times, these thoughts that we want to become aware of so that we may interrupt, and eventually change them to suit exactly what we are after. Once you can do this, you will never wake up on the wrong side of the bed again, in fact you will be able to control your moods, your emotions, your energy levels, and ultimately your life.

It is time to start to examine those thoughts as they happen and begin learning how to listen to what is being said. The most important reason for this is that these thoughts are where all the clues lie to discovering the negative resistance in your life and how they shape your feelings toward external events. You will probably find that most of the thoughts you are having are negative, and usually based on doom and gloom scenarios that create a wave of elevating emotional responses causing you to behave in a certain manner. For example, if you wake up in the morning and the first thing you do is get an email regarding something you messed up at work, then immediately after entering the shower your STP will sound a lot like this: 'I can't believe I messed that up — maybe they found out that I'm not as capable as they thought I was. What if they think I'm not right for the job? I bet you it was Peter who ratted me out. I've always known he would stab me in the back. I should have listened to Mary that day warning me about him. 'What if he tells them about that other time I forgot to send out that package on time?''. One STP after another, creating an emotional state that will determine your mood and behaviour.

Knowing what you know now, you can see that all these thoughts are based on what we learned in the first principle, and that you are responding to them based on your beliefs, fears, and the sum of all your past experiences. Without your awareness and active involvement, you are setting yourself up for a day full of anxiety, and one where your actions will be based on those thoughts instead of the actual facts. In this case of the shower example I gave above, the fact may be that there was just a simple misunderstanding that can be easily resolved, and it is fixed and over as soon as you get into the office. But, if you've worked yourself up and you go in and start accusing people or acting defensive, you could create a real problem for yourself.

Imagine how many situations could have turned out completely different if you had altered your thoughts and had a positive, controlled mind. You would always make the right decisions and would always be in a peak state allowing you to spend more time feeling great, confident, and in control of achieving your goals.

Master Training

1. Notice STPs, and write them down. (20 minutes to complete)

Grab a pen and paper, or use the space below, and find a place where you can sit quietly without interruptions. Once there, I want you to find something in the room, or the park, or wherever you may be at this time, to focus on. It could be a picture on the wall, a tree, a cloud — anything that is in your comfortable field of vision.

Once you are ready and have chosen your object, I want you to begin thinking about that object. Actively engage in thought about whatever it is you have chosen to focus on. For example, let's say you choose a car that happens to be parked outside your home that you can see through your living room window. Really look at the car and think about all the different aspects of it. For example: "That's a nice car. The car is blue. I think it might be a BMW, or an Audi. It's parked under the big oak tree in the front. I think it belongs to the neighbors. The car has tinted windows." Note that you can think about anything that you want, as long as it is relevant to the object that you are focusing on. But, as a guide, start by using its appearance to form thoughts, and then move to anything related to it. As you do this for a minute or two, you will discover that your mind will naturally wander to other thoughts and ideas. This is what we want to be aware of.

Your goal is to focus until your subconscious mind begins spewing out chatter. Let it happen but become aware of it. You may have to start over a couple times, but each time try and catch the thoughts that eventually lead you away from the thing you are focusing on.

2. Think of two occurrences where you reacted emotionally to an event.

- What were the events?

- What was the emotion or reaction?

- What were the underlying STPs?

- If you didn't have those STPs would you have behaved differently?

- What beliefs or ideals does your subconscious mind have programmed that caused you to have these STPs?

PRINCIPLE 3

THE MIND-BODY CONNECTION

Do you remember when you were in grade school, perhaps grade one or two, and in order to ask a question you were required to raise your arm in the air? Do you also remember forming a single file line when gearing up to enter the gym for an assembly or even just to get into your classroom? I'm pretty sure that most of you can recall a memory like this as far back as elementary school, and if you are unable to recall it, you are still very aware of this process occurring at some point in those early childhood years. This is basic cultural programming, and because you now understand how the mind works you can clearly see why this process was so important. What you may not know is that not only is it subconscious mind programming, it is also bringing in body programming, making it an extremely powerful behavioural program that becomes ingrained in your mind-body self.

The idea of the mind-body connection is nothing new, and studies have shown that this is not only a real thing, but has been used with incredible effectiveness to affect behavioural responses in human beings. The reason it's so powerful is that not only is the mind influencing the body, but the body can also influence the mind. The point you need to take from this is that your mind and your body are in fact two parts of a whole. Your mind is more than just the region of your head that you perceive as the centre of your thoughts. In fact, the only reason you think this is because four of your most prominent senses — your vision, hearing, sense of smell, and taste — happen to take place in this region and therefore give you the 'feeling' that your thoughts are only in your head.

"According to the mind-body or biopsychosocial paradigm, which supersedes the older biomedical model, there is no real division between mind and body because of networks of communication that exist between the brain and neurological, endocrine and immune systems."

—Oakley Ray, Professor Emeritus of Psychology, Psychiatry and Pharmacology at Vanderbilt University (Nashville, TN, USA).

Neuroscience has discovered that some of the commands that you presume start in your brain *actually* start in other areas of your body. When you really think about it, this makes perfect sense, as the nervous system that spans your entire body is linked to your brain.

Now, I'm not going to go into a lengthy scientific explanation, I just wanted you to see that this connection is, in fact, happening and let you know that for the remainder of this manifesto we will refer to this mind and body connection as the "mind-body". This understanding will allow you to become even more aware of your habitual behaviours and learn how to disengage unwanted connections and build new, empowering ones that will have a profound impact on your life.

This knowledge has been known in eastern cultures for centuries, well before the discovery of the Americas, and what used to be considered outlying forms of medicine — such as acupuncture or yoga — have become part of our mainstream wellness solutions. The underlying use of these treatments, however, has been known and used by governments, the military, and the media since managing people's behaviours become an essential part of our socio-economic model of life. Realizing this will allow you to radically change your own feelings and behaviour solely based on how you use your body.

Before we examine the hidden cultural mind-body programs that most people experience daily, let's review some of the more common connections that you are probably already aware of, yet have not fully dissected to your benefit. One simple example of a mind-body connection that has become almost pandemic in the western world is that of depression.

(Please note that my goal here is to identify the mind-body connection that is a part of this diagnosis and not to imply that depression is simply a result of this phenomenon. It is more complex than that, and involves many other factors, however, there is a clear-cut relationship between the mind and the body, each part affecting the other creating a circle of emotional responses that make depression a perfect example of how this mind-body functions.)

I lived in London for a time, and while there I had the pleasure of attending *Anthony Robbins: Unleash the Power Within.* It was an incredible three-day event filled with high energy, positivity, and motivational masterclasses. It was exactly what I was looking for as a young nightclub owner hoping to take my business and success to the next level. It's where I was first introduced to this mind-body connection, and where I began to really understand the power of physiology. So much so that I was able to not just experience Tony using this tool to help someone with depression, but also how Tony himself used the tool throughout his entire program to influence the emotional state of those attending. As a master of this phenomenon, he took everyone in that venue through a carefully orchestrated experience using a variety of powerful techniques, one being this mind-body connection.

Tony talked directly to an audience member who had been experiencing depression and suicidal thoughts and was unable to break free from its grip. The person in the audience showed clear physiological signs of depression, which can be identified by even the most untrained eye — lowered head, shallow breath, soft voice, frowned facial features, constant sighs, eyes focused down, etc. There are obvious physical characteristics that come with being in a state of depression, and Tony highlighted this fact perfectly. In fact, pretty much every feeling that we have has a corresponding physical projection which can be mapped and identified, allowing us to more easily identify someone else's internal subjective experience. This is why 80% of human communication has nothing to do with what's coming out of the mouth.

Once Tony had called our attention to the fact that there was a clear relationship between the mind and body, he revealed that we can change our behaviour, not by focusing on the mind alone, but by also focusing on our bodies. This is what Tony did with the audience member. He distracted the person by using a pattern interruption technique which allowed him to manipulate their physiological condition and, in turn, change how they felt.

By instigating a programmed physiological response that is tied to laughter, he took that person from feeling depressed to feeling good in a matter of seconds. Immediately, the subject's body language went from that of a depressed person, to one that had a smile, held their head up, eyes up, shoulders relaxed, and took on the physiology of a happy person. Though it only lasted for a few moments, what Tony was demonstrating is that you cannot be depressed if your body is exhibiting the programmed relational physiology of a happy person and, in the reverse, a person exhibiting the physical attributes of a depressed person cannot feel happy.

I want you to try this experiment, so you can experience this powerful truth for yourself and see how your body has an equal weight in how you think, and ultimately how you feel.

Sit back in your chair and smile as big as you can. You know how to do it — I'm not asking you to be happy or feel anything at this moment — I just want you to simply put a massive grin on your face and hold it for one minute. The secret is holding it for the entire minute. Pay attention to your thoughts and especially how you begin to feel. Do you find it kind of silly? Are you laughing to yourself? Notice that what you can't do is feel bad while you hold that smile! You may want to, but in order for that to happen you would have to stop smiling!

Smiling is related to good feelings, so during this exercise your mind will produce thoughts related to that body command despite your efforts to think otherwise. Of course, if your habitual frame of reference is feeling crappy, it will be very easy for your mind to signal your body to stop smiling and return to a shittier way of being, however, with practice, smiling on purpose despite the will of your subconscious programming will maintain your good feelings. This is a powerful tool, and at the end of this step, I will give you some exercises that will enable you to add this knowledge to the rest of the program so that you have an armada of powerful techniques to re-invent your mind-body self!

So, now we understand the connection between our mind and our body and, with a little bit of retrospection, we can see that many of our feelings and thoughts are tied to an interrelated physiological state. With enough practice, this will allow you to turn on a dime from negative to positive feelings and behaviours, freeing you from the programmed default responses that you have been experiencing till now. Using your skills of self-awareness that you learnt in the second principle, and now learning to also be aware of your body language is just the beginning of the path to discovering the power within. Already, you can see the power it holds and now, when we discuss the larger, cultural, mind-body programs that you are a part of, you will you be able to fully grasp the incredible power this knowledge holds for you!

At the beginning of this step, I asked you to remember a time when you raised your hand in school. You can see how this repetitive physical program, along with the thought process of 'requiring permission from an authoritative figure' becomes engrained in the subconscious mind, so much so that even to this day I'm sure there are times when you have raised your hand to get permission for one thing or another. In fact, if you raise your hand right now you will probably get a feeling of vulnerability, conformity, and giving up power. But, it will feel like okay too. This is how you were programmed to feel so that you, along with the general populace, would learn to respect and obey authoritative figures. We can also re-examine the process of lining up in school. This too was programming to prepare you to conform to the expectations of the socio-economic system. This one is easy to identify in your adult life because you subconsciously line up when required without anyone directing you, and if someone attempts to break this cultural programming you will immediately make them aware of the 'lineup'. Not only will you line up, but you will also likely keep to yourself and not engage in chatter with those around you. This was frowned upon in the school line, therefore, most people are afraid to engage with another human being that is standing less than two feet away from them. I'm not arguing the validity or the necessity to create cultural programs, all I am saying is that it is happening to you, and you need to know why so that you can be aware of the thoughts and emotions that are tied to these types of programmed mind-body behaviours.
Understanding this will ensure that you are in control of your own mind, are able to question the validity of circumstances, and can react appropriately with your own free will.

Let me give you one more programmed example. Have you ever held your hand to your chest when you sing the national anthem? This simple gesture is relationally tied to feelings of patriotism, pride, and significance, and its aim is to bind together a people in common values. What you can now see is how this can easily be used to manipulate the masses. Your subconscious mind-body self will react to this stimulus releasing powerful emotional thoughts and feelings of patriotism. Just get our leader to hold his hand to his chest and proclaim war on another country and you will be a conforming subject. Hold that hand up with a straight arm slightly above eye level and you can be convinced to eliminate a race!

The mind-body connection is powerful — understand this power and use it to create a kind, compassionate, healthy, wealthy, new you!

Master Training

1. Identify and list three mind-body programs that you are actively entertaining subconsciously.

2. Notice an unwanted STP that is persisting. How is your body behaving just before that thought arises? Are you breathing heavy, are you tense in the shoulders, etc.? Write it down!

3. List three physiological things that you can do when you are in a negative thought pattern or feeling down.

Exercise:

Think of something that makes you scared — spiders, mice, flying, anything! Notice what your body does and write down a minimum of four ways it is reacting to this thought. If you start to become uncomfortable with this thought process, then close your eyes and just imagine yourself floating above, almost like a floating drone camera, watching your own reaction. Notice how you're behaving. Focus on your body language — your eyes, your legs, your muscles, your breathing — and be an impartial observer.

4 things your body does when scared

1_____

2_____

3_____

4_____

Now, I want you to do the same exercise, except this time I want you to imagine a time when you were feeling incredibly happy, peaceful, and alive! No need to be an observer in this one, just close your eyes and go there in your mind. How is your body behaving now?

4 things your body does when happy

1_____

2_____

3_____

4_____

Now comes the fun part! I call this the Happy Body Blitz!

I want you to look at the four things your body did when you were happy, and I want you to start putting your body in that same configuration. Do all those things that you listed and this time I want you to think about the thing that scares you while you maintain your body in those four happy ways.

Try it now.

Keep your body aligned in happy-mode for up 10 seconds. Then take a deep breath and sigh.

Did you notice how your fear of the thing that scares you reduced substantially? If you could rate your fear from 1 to 10; 10 being terror, what was the rating before, and after this simple exercise?

Do this exercise a few times and notice your fear level. Does it drop? Stay the same? Between every attempt, close your eyes and go back to your happy moment and immerse yourself in those wonderful mind-body feelings before repeating the Happy Body Blitz. As you become more comfortable, increase the length of time from 10 seconds to 30 seconds.

With practice, you will soon no longer be scared when you think about what scares you. In fact, your mind will probably start to naturally drift away from those negative STPs that you have about your fear!

This is a great way to use your physiology to change your unwanted STPs!

PRINCIPLE 4

THE POWER OF GIVE (GOALS, IMAGINATION, VISUALIZATION, EXPECTATION)

What do you want?

Not the easiest of questions to answer now, is it?

Maybe you have always had an idea about what you really want but if you've been reading and absorbing the new insights over the last three principles, perhaps you may be questioning what it is you really want to do. It might seem now that what you think you want was actually programmed into your mind, and your thought processes created an ideal goal to meet this programming, and created STPs that led you to want or desire a certain something.

What if your goal is not based on *what you really want* but instead it is a programming outcome from your subconscious mind which is protecting you from certain fears or painful emotions?

Think about it.

Imagine that your goal is to achieve the highest position in your company. Maybe that goal isn't what you really want, but was created because you have always feared not being good enough or not fitting in, and by being the big boss you would no longer have to face those concerns. Hmmm. On the other hand, if your goal is to be an actor or singer, perhaps this is also a response to the programming embedded in your subconscious.

What I'm proposing is that everything you do is directly related to your thinking. You might say, "Well of course it is! I was raised and experienced life which led me to have these goals and desires!" And yes, that makes logical sense, right? But, it's not just the things you can consciously remember that have shaped who you are, there are so many other unconscious factors that had a part to play. Remember that you are not YOU, but a YOU that up to this point was being guided by a default programming that we are trying to free you from. This is the reason why, at a certain point in life, people get curious or anxious and feel that there is something missing — that they want purpose in life.

I want to be clear that my aim here is not to scare you into thinking that you're a robot, but what I am offering is the knowledge that you can change any and all of this programming and re-create your life. If it is more money that you're after, then we can create the kind of thinking, the right kind of STP, that will take you to that goal. If you experienced different programming in your past you would have different results in your life PERIOD. So, right now what we want to do is contemplate our goals and understand why we have them, and if they align with what we truly want.

The next step in uncovering our most authentic goals is to ask a few simple questions. First, ask yourself if what you want is the end result, or is it the means.

This is very important to identify, because without making the differentiation, you will not feel the wonderful ecstasy of accomplishment when you smash those goals. Instead, there will be an empty feeling and a yearning for more. It is why so many 'accomplished' people seem to self-destruct despite being on a culturally accepted pedestal of achievement. We now know that, more often than not, that pedestal is not their own.

A common example is a goal of having money. Many people are driven to have money, and why wouldn't they be?! It has become the foundation of our society. Money, however, is a poor man's goal. Think about it — money is just a rectangular paper that is printed with patterns and faces of some generally accepted famous people. Why would you want to have a lot of this printed paper? Sounds like a stupid thing to ask right — but it isn't. Your end goal is not having money, it's what you get with the money, and I'm not talking about the material things, I'm talking about the feelings and emotions you get. That's the ultimate goal — the feelings that will come with wealth. In this case, money is the means, not the goal.

Things are the means, jobs are the means, careers are the means, and businesses are the means. These are not your goals, these are the stepping stones to your goals. This is important because just the change in language, the change in the classification, will allow your mind to overcome certain mental blocks, as well as ensuring you don't feel deflated when you get the means. Instead, you will relish being closer to realizing your life's true desires.

This is a fundamental key to your success. The reclassification of your current goals will interrupt your subconscious programming and make it easier for you to attain all those means, be it money, property, or businesses, that you may have found difficult in the past. Now they will become easier, aligned, and effortless.

The next question to ask yourself is if your goal, or stepping stone, is something that *you* solely want, or it is being influenced by others. Are you alone in the process, or is a circumstance or person steering you in the direction of the goal?

It is important to really reflect and contemplate this question. If what you are working towards is not your vision, then you will never be satisfied and more than likely end up back in a place where you are searching for more out of life. This is your path and although others may be a part of it, it is yours and yours alone to create, to pursue, and to share when the time is right.

I cannot count the number of times I have witnessed people make goals because they thought it was the right thing to do based on someone else's expectations (either direct expectations or implied expectations) not because it was their own dream.

It's like the guy who wants to quit smoking because his wife is consistently demanding that he quits. He will seek out all the help he can get to accomplish this goal, yet he will continue to smoke in secret and ultimately return to the habit which he himself proclaimed was done for good. He never wanted to quit, or he wasn't ready to quit on those terms. Subconsciously, the goals and dreams created by the need to please others are doomed to failure, and if not failure than to no satisfaction upon completion.

Let me clarify a few things. There is no harm in shared goals, and those can be rewarding and exciting to explore, however, they must be aligned with your own personal goals in order to become something that your subconscious mind can get behind. So, there must be a personal congruence within you in order to get excited and inspired about your goals. This is not available when you think it's what you should do, and if you do what you should do, you will never do what you want to do!

I want you to understand this concept fully before we move on to the next section, because with it will come the ability to gain momentum by easily achieving those stepping stones that will get you to your goal. When you understand that your goal is a feeling, an emotional state, you can begin feeling those emotions while you work on your steps. When you achieve your goal, which is more of those feelings, than you can create more steps, and your life becomes magical and always filled with the right type of emotional bliss. When you master this system, you will be able to create a purpose-driven life filled with abundance. You will be the master of everything.

What goals do you have right now?

What feelings or emotions will achieving those goals give you?

What can you do right now to achieve those feelings and emotions?

Now, from this point on, we are going to change the word 'goal' to 'step'. Goals are now the feelings we are after.

So, what 'steps' could you create that will move you toward having more and more of those feelings (goals)?

What steps excite you about the future?

What steps do you have for yourself right now?

Notice how you have less resistance when you call them steps!?

Are these steps your own?

When you imagine achieving these steps do you feel that they satisfy the feeling and emotions that YOU are searching for?

The next component of this process is IMAGINATION and one of my favourite topics in this entire manifesto. Not only is it a component of the GIVE process but it is also one of the most powerful tools you possess as a wonderful and divine human being. The power of the imagination is beyond words, although I will try and make it as obvious to you as I possibly can so that you may understand the incredible gift that it is! It is the grand master, the grand creator and if you believe in God, or a higher power, than this is your link to them. This is how you create your own life like a god!

What makes imagination so incredibly powerful that it moves me to associate it with the likes of the creator; whoever that may be to you, and proclaim it as the link to communicate with them? Well, let's start by using the words of a more land-based, mortal subject like Albert Einstein.

"I am enough of an artist to draw freely upon my imagination. Imagination is more important than knowledge. Knowledge is limited. Imagination encircles the world."

Nothing in the known physical world was created without first being imagined in the mind of a fellow human being. This is a truly powerful link that gets little attention. Think about it, without imagination even the simplest things you take for granted on a daily basis would have been IMPOSSIBLE. Your car, your phone, your bathroom, your toothbrush, literally everything that exists in our external physical world had to first arise as a thought in the imagination of man or woman, and then manifested and constructed into reality. Even the ideas around today that seem so far-fetched and impossible, like the teleportation of matter, have already begun to be developed.

Creation is not born of external processes; it is born in the minds of humans and then eventually manifested into reality. So, in essence, the birthplace of all things begins in the mind, in the imagination, in you! This is the real 'big bang' baby! Because even the theories and discoveries proposed in science today were born in the incredibly powerful gift that each and everyone one of us possesses — the imagination. It is a gift so incredibly powerful, so immense, that it has been downplayed to you since you began attending grade school. The imagination to you, and to most people, is child's play. In fact, those that displayed excess imagination as young children were usually coerced into becoming less creative and usually labelled with disorders such as ADHD or OCD. Imagination was good for

38

a little while, but as you become part of society you were expected to get your shit together and conform. How dare you daydream in class — pay attention to what I'm saying to you!

Now, this amazing power of creation, the amazing gift of imagination, has been cleverly kidnapped from even the youngest minds through the use of tablets, phones, and tv's, because with these digital devices you no longer need to use your imagination. It is fabricated for you in magnificent colours, with magnificent characters, and in magnificent stories, none of which you imagined yourself. It is vital that you understand how powerful this is, and how ineffective these children will be at creating a magical life for themselves. They will be unable to fathom new ideas, new scenarios, and new paths. Instead, they will be perfectly conformed, never fulfilled, yet never truly understanding why. It is your responsibility to encourage the use of this power, the power of imagination, while you are still able to access it. This is not a conspiracy debate, and I am not here to evaluate whether this was purposely programmed to limit the imagination of society. No, I am simply here to expand your awareness and introduce you to an ingredient that will allow you to design your own reality and those of your children. Now that we understand how all things in our physical reality were first created in the imagination, we can make the connection and use it to create the things that we truly want in our lives. If we are unable to imagine what we want, then we can never create it in the real world. Therefore, this is such an amazing tool because most people don't actually imagine themselves having achieved their goals. I'm not talking about visualisation, that is yet to come, what I am talking about is 'make believe'!

Just for a moment, I want you to travel back in time in your mind and remember when you were a child and were playing. Maybe you were pretending to drink tea with your dolls and stuffed toys, or pretending you and your friends were flying a ship through space battling alien forces — whatever scenario comes to mind will do. This was called 'make believe', aka imagination! Remember how you made it feel real, and how you played your part perfectly, acting out the scene in your external physical world as if you were actually experiencing it. You could almost taste the tea, almost feel the rush of being chased by aliens, you were immersed in a reality that was created in your mind, in your imagination. Now, think about the last time you imagined something, the last time you created an exciting adventure in your mind. What was it?

Before we continue, let's pause and identify the right type of imagination and the default STP type of imagination. You do, in fact, imagine all the time, however, it is not guided or purposeful, it is based on subconscious thought processes (STPs) and happens without your direct control. That type of imagination is usually comprised of impending doom and involves future events where you anticipate undesirable outcomes due to perceived lack of control, leading your mind to construct worst-case scenarios creating anxiety and dread. However, now through self-awareness you are able to see how and why these thoughts and visions occur and can easily label them as such. So, in essence, the imagination we are after at this time is the directed, on purpose, type of imagination — a created scenario of make believe that we choose consciously. We will call this 'positive and playful' imagination and we will use it throughout this manifesto in various principles to give us real power over our minds, our thoughts and, ultimately, our reality.

The power of imagination works in a couple of ways; first, it is the creative power behind all physical reality. Like I mentioned previously, nothing has ever been created without it first being imagined. Secondly, the mind cannot differentiate between what is real, or what is imagined. We know this to be true by logically contemplating a phobia or fear we may hold. No matter how much someone has convinced you that there is no logical need to fear a spider, your mind creates feelings and responses in line with your imagined fear. These two rules are the driving force behind the power that imagination plays in the programming of our mind, our body, and finally our reality. So much so, that it does more for behavioural change than any logical reasoning ever will. You can't logically think your way out of addiction, but with imagination you can bypass logic and affect the subconscious mind, which governs your every move based on its programming.

So, how do you use imagination to design your life?
Well, you simply imagine a scenario in your mind where you have already accomplished your steps, achieved your goal, and have started planning the next steps. You create a future in your mind of living a day having already completed various steps and having achieved the immense feelings that were your goal. Let yourself go wild and imagine all the great things you would be doing, the reactions of those around you, the new opportunities and possibilities. Also, imagine what else you would be planning and what

new steps you might have. This is a creative process, so allow yourself to run wild as long as you are true to your desires, and keep all the imagery and feelings positive and exciting. You may even discover new steps that you hadn't even thought of before until now! Allow your creative mind to take you on a fantastical journey, where new insights about your desires will naturally manifest as you build imagination momentum.

Let's take a moment now to recap, and perform some exercises, so that we can fully understand the first two components in the Power of GIVE.

GOALS

Example goal: Feeling of self-worth, significance, or purpose. Remember that 'goals' are feelings that you want to have when you achieve your steps.

Steps to get to this goal:

- Increase my business by 25%
- Complete my book
- Engage in physical activity 3 x week
- Attain recognition in my field at the award ceremony

IMAGINATION

Imagine yourself walking up to receive an award for your work and notice how accomplished you feel. Imagine the room and what the tables look like. Imagine having a copy of your book on the table where you are having dinner and how wonderful you feel for having completed it. Go to the bathroom and imagine running into people. Notice what they are wearing and saying to you. Look at yourself in the mirror and realise how much leaner you look. Stare at yourself and smile, thinking about what new opportunities lay ahead.

There are only a few rules in the imagination part of this exercise:

- Do not bring into your imagination people that you dislike.
- Do not imagine feelings of revenge.
- Keep it positive and about your STEPS.
- Make sure you imagine creating new STEPS for the future.
- Notice all the details — the type of music playing, the weather, colour of tablecloths, carpet etc.

The third component of GIVE is VISUALIZATION, and although it can be classified as a type of imagination, it is a very specific and focused type of imagination that requires its own mastery and hence is its own component. Only once we are able to create imaginary flow in our minds can we purposely create the right kind of focused imagination called 'visualization'

This tool will help you bring an imagined scenario into reality faster than a speeding bullet, yet without all the other components it loses its effectiveness, hence why the whole of this process is where the power to create the life you desire lies. This powerful GIVE technique is a wonderful vehicle, and If imagination is the fuel, visualization is the steering wheel!

Throughout this manifesto so far, you have learned that your thoughts create your reality, and you were able to logically comprehend how this occurs from a personal standpoint but also from a cultural, and societal standpoint. For example, the saying 'early bird gets the worm' stems from a belief that has been programmed into our corporate culture so much so, that conflicting beliefs are not only frowned upon but alienated regardless of the 'reality'. Creating a focused vision, without either first reprogramming our beliefs or ensuring their alignment, will result in our subconscious mind rejecting the vision and sabotaging it. Visualization works on these assumptions, allowing you to perceive exactly what it is you want to be doing at some point in the future in accordance with your beliefs.

Knowing what you want via the creation of your steps and goals, along with the ability to imagine the euphoria of their accomplishment, and to be able to understand what areas you can focus on to ensure your visualization is in line with those cultural/societal beliefs, makes this process an incredibly powerful tool. To put it in layman's terms, you can now harness the power of focused imagination (visualization) knowing what the future should consist of based on your culturally programmed expectations.

Let's take one of the steps listed in the GOAL example above to break down the process and create a visualization sequence that will allow you to create the desired outcome in your own life. Let's take 'increasing sales by 25%'. Someone who has achieved the steps of increasing the sales in their business will have certain characteristics that will allow you to model their behaviour in your mind's eye and replicate it. So, by answering a few simple questions you can create a visualization that is congruent with a person that, in your mind, would be capable of achieving a 25% increase in their business.

Visual Exercise 1

Imagine a person who owns a business and has consistently achieved sales increases of over 25%, delivering a substantial increase in net profits. Close your eyes and see this person going about a day in their lives. Imagine that you could know what they think and say.

What type of TV shows would this person watch?

What words would this person use when talking?

What would this person do when faced with challenges and setbacks?

How much time would they spend watching TV?

What activities would this person be involved in?

What would they wear?

What would their body movements look like when they are walking, talking, laughing etc.?

How would this person react to situations they cannot control?

How would this person feel?

How do YOU feel about this person?

Do you like this person that you see?

Now that you have answered the questions you can use your answers to create a realistic visualization of yourself in the future and you can also see that in order to become that type of person, you will need to have similar thoughts and behaviours that accompany that type of result. If you are unable to envision yourself in this future it could be because your current beliefs and values are contradicting what you now know is required to be that type of person, and will sabotage you at every opportunity.

Let's look at another scenario. Imagine someone who wants to be rich, who wants to have a better life with a great house, great car, holiday homes, and the lot, yet their subconscious programming is rooted with a belief that money is evil, and that rich people are selfish. No matter how much visualization this person attempts, it will never yield the desired result because their programmed beliefs are not in-line with that of a wealthy person. Therefore, imagining someone else having those things and answering the questions will highlight any programming that will need to be changed to achieve these desires.

Now that you have established that you are aligned with your vision you can actively visualize yourself in a future scenario of having accomplished your step. To do this you will need to first practice on purpose by setting aside some time every day to visualise your future self. Eventually, you will be able to hold this visual in your mind throughout your daily life, always aware of your goal, always attentive to your thoughts and actions, always monitoring your thoughts. Which leads us to…

Visual Exercise 2

Visualize yourself in the future already having achieved your step. Visualise what a day in your life would be like. Use the questions from that Visual Exercise 1, but apply them to your own life, and your own step. Visualise yourself doing those things and behaving in that manner. See yourself talking to people, using the right words, noticing your body movements and how they are positive and confident. Notice the details, and once you're finished, go through it again in your mind with your eyes open, and write down everything you see. Use as many specifics as possible such as:

- The colors of things.
- The type of clothing and shoes you wore.
- The taste of something you ate or drank.
- The temperature in the room.
- The sounds in the room.
- The feel of your surroundings.
- How were you feeling?
- Did you find any STPs that made you feel that it was not realistic?
- What were the beliefs, or thoughts, that made you question it becoming reality?

44

Re-program those beliefs so they align with your desires and do the exercise again! (See Principle 7 for more information on removing limiting beliefs and reprogramming the mind-body.)

Now, I'm going to introduce you to a hidden knowledge, a hidden process, that turns your visualizations into incredibly powerful tools for creating your new life. This knowledge will probably test one of your programmed beliefs as most people will have never had the opportunity to learn it, let alone make it a part of their thinking process. Before I begin, I need to explain what that current belief is, and remind you that it is a belief and nothing more.

The programmed belief is *linear time*.

Yes, that's right, past, present and future — linear time. No, this is not as crazy as it sounds and in order for most of you to accept it, I have chosen to refer to the currently accepted theory of space-time, so that this small tidbit of knowledge will allow you to use this process without having to re-program your limiting beliefs around linear time. Furthermore, it will allow you to time travel using your mind.

Linear time is simply a method of counting that we have devised to depict change, be it physical or in the conscious realm. All it truly is, is a measurement tool for change. This has been discussed by philosophers and scientists throughout history, and it continues to be a sensitive topic today — especially with the advancements made in quantum physics. In fact, it's because we perceive things as having a beginning and an end (past, present, and future) that we need to have an explanation for how it all started. Without the linear time model, we would not fear death, and we would not feel as if TIME was something slipping away —our perception of our reality would be completely different. This tool called "time" is also known as the fourth dimension, and is not as linear as you have been taught to believe!

Quantum physics proposes that any and all events (or change) are a possibility right up until we actively observe it, (focus our attention on it) and only then does it materialize into our reality. Have you heard of the thought experiment known as Schrodinger's cat? If you have then you can comprehend the strange world of quantum physics (if you haven't, I explain it below) and, although you or I may never be able to explain it in an equation, all we need to understand is that this is happening, and knowing how to use it to supercharge the effects of visualization remains the number one goal of this section. Besides, I think even quantum physicists struggle to make sense of the endless array of possibilities, and along with that, they too are 'imagining' unfathomable theories in order to solve their precious equations.

For those of you that have never learned about the Schrodinger's cat experiment, here is a brief explanation. Schrodinger, a scientist, placed a living cat in a box which had been fitted with a device that contained a radioactive material that released a deadly poison that the cat would breathe in and die. The catch, however, was that the type of radioactive material was known to be unstable and there was no way to predict if the poison was actually released when activated. Once he placed the cat in the box, he closed the lid and activated the radioactive mechanism never knowing if the poison would be released and kill the cat. He had no way of knowing whether the cat was dead or alive until he opened the box and observed the outcome. Since he did not know the outcome before he opened the box, he proposed that in that moment the cat was both dead, and alive! Both outcomes were possible, both were suspended in a wave of possibility, yet only when he revealed the true outcome would it materialize into reality. This, along with other repeatable experiments, proves that time (the measurement of change events) is not what we commonly think it is. It also demonstrates that events that we believe are part of the past, present, or future, are actually entangled. So, not only can you affect the future, but you can also affect the past. Events can be affected in reverse, or more accurately, in a cycle or circle of possibilities. Past, present, and future are change events happening in a circle and affecting each other regardless of the direction they are moving in. The most important thing for you to understand here is that every single possibility in your life is available and that all outcomes are possible, and may have already occurred despite your stranglehold on the fact that what is happening right now is what you consider to be the present.

You're probably wondering 'how is this going to help me?' Well, this weird little gem of a concept will allow you to visualize in a manner that not only reprograms your subconscious, but it will also direct your reality toward a specific outcome that is possible, and available right now. We can manipulate the mind to focus on the desired outcome, and hence turn it into reality. It's like using our mind to materialize a living cat so that when we open the box door, the cat is always alive. We choose! And we choose by using my *Time Loop* method!

Here comes the beautiful part of it all. You don't even really need to believe me, or the greatest minds in science for that matter. All you really have to do is imagine the process and it will work for you regardless. I mentioned earlier that the subconscious mind cannot differentiate between what is real, and what is imagined. So, luckily for you, this part only requires your ability to pretend, which of course you already know how to do. Trust me when I say that if you follow the Time Loop exercise, you will begin to see the results and begin to believe, resulting in an even more powerful tool that allows you to create your life on purpose.

Now, I want you to imagine a bicycle wheel. One with countless metal spokes connecting the centre of the wheel to the inside rim. The rim and wheel form a circle that represents time. The centre of the wheel, where the spokes originate, is you. Imagine yourself in the centre of a massive wheel and look out and see a portion of the spokes and part of the rim or wheel in the distance. By turning your head in either direction you can see more spokes and a different section of the wheel in the distance — a different section of time. I want you to imagine that each spoke is a portal to a particular time, and by traveling down that spoke in your mind you can access that specific moment in time, whether it be in the past or in the future, and you can send or receive information from your current present position. Your current position in the centre is your *now* moment, which is the only real moment of reality that we have. Each now moment is sent down a portal and logged in the wheel of time. Since it is a circle there is no 'identifiable' beginning or end and hence why this thought experiment can allow your mind to influence your reality.

I'm going to give you an example from my own life and use it to show you how I was able to manipulate my subconscious and create a past that exponentially strengthened my ability to mould my life into exactly what I wanted. I did this by visualizing myself at a particular moment in the past, sending and receiving information, and then visualising myself in the future and doing the same. This process takes time to learn and to master, but once you do, you will gain powerful insights that allow you to affect your subconscious in such a way that it will create your desired outcomes easily and effortlessly. I'm going to use the example of writing this manifesto, and how I purposely made this 'step' possible by using the visualization techniques we discussed and in particular this *Time Loop* system.

Most mornings I hit the gym at 8 am and, after my warm-up stretch, I usually like to get on the elliptical machine for 30 minutes of cardio. I never turn on the tv screen, in fact, I find that seeing my own reflection makes it easier for me to access the Time Loop and communicate with myself. So, the first thing I do is choose the step that I will be working on and bring that into my mind, in this case it was the completion of this manifesto. I start off by recalling a time in my past where I was making bad choices and struggling with a certain issue and I go there in my mind, as if I have time travelled there and am watching and witnessing the events through a camera. I then remember the thoughts and state I was in at that particular time, and I begin to formulate a thought that if I had had at that time would have empowered me to get me to where I am today.

Here is what I planted...

It's ok that I made this choice, I'm learning from it and I know that I will get stronger the next time. These poor choices and struggles are important for me because I will be able to use these experiences to help others. I'm not going to be hard on myself, instead I am going to try and listen to my future self for guidance. Even though I can't see it right now, I know that if I continue to try that I will eventually overcome these issues. I'm not going to be hard on myself, instead I am going to be more aware of the things I do and use them to move forward to a better life. I can hear my future self, a little voice in the back of my mind, like a guardian angel trying to help me, never judging, always there with love and trust. Even if I falter I am becoming more connected and learning to be strong.

In the present I have already overcome the issues, however, I am reinforcing the result and guiding my past self toward this present. Now if you really want to go down the rabbit hole with me you can think about how it was this 'present me', which is really the 'future me' since I'm inside my past self, that actually created this particular present. If I hadn't messaged myself in the past than I would have never overcome those issues. Mind blown, right!? Even deeper is the fact that when I now think about those past struggles, I CAN ACTUALLY REMEMBER HEARING A GUIDING VOICE!

I do this for about 10 minutes, and I know that I have been effective because when I look at the digital display on the elliptical machine, though

10 minutes have passed I feel like it was only two minutes. When I first started using this tool I was shocked at how much time is distorted, and why wouldn't it be? Your mind is in essence 'time travelling'. This time distortion phenomenon is your clue that you are doing it correctly and effectively! It is so distorted that I always do this visualization Time Loop when I do cardio because it doesn't feel like a struggle to do 30 minutes of exercise — so many benefits!

Using this Time Loop method is the key to visualization and will dramatically improve the quality of your life. Unlike most other manifestation techniques that are available today, using this process will not only penetrate your subconscious mind — the director of all your thoughts and habits — it will also align your past, present, and future so that everything that has ever happened to you was leading you to the future that you have now created in your mind. This will change how you feel about past events that maybe you previously thought of as regretful or bad, and enable you to see how they were just events that were actually guiding you to where you are now — a place where you can actively design the future that you truly want. It gives you back total control over your life, and gives you the power to never blame people, circumstances, or any external factors for the negative events in your life. You are now the creator of your life, the master of your destiny!

Let's review everything that you have learned so far with the power of GIVE and lay them out step by step so that you can clearly see the process and use it effectively and efficiently to design your life.

GOALS

- Set your ultimate goals based on your search for *feelings and emotional needs*.
- Create 'steps' to reach those goals and write them down. Start with a list of three short and three long-term steps that encompass your current desires, and are also aligned with your ultimate goals.

IMAGINATION

- Make believe, fantasize, daydream about what life might be like if you had achieved those steps, and were already experiencing the feelings and emotions of your goals. This is a *no limit imagination period* much like a child's make-believe session.

Picture every fantastic possibility and feel those feelings of joy and happiness!

VISUALISATION

- Now it's time to *focus your imagination* and create a realistic scenario based on your previous fantasy. First, visualise someone who has already achieved the 'step' that you are working on and go back to the section where you can use the correct techniques to maximise this process. Secondly, visualise yourself as that person and, in your mind, experience an event as that person. Remember to notice your interior STPs and reprogram any limiting beliefs.
- *Time Loop*: Once you have visualised your step, you can begin to send and receive information, travelling through time, embracing the past, imprinting new thoughts, and guiding your life in the direction you want.

Take some time to review this section before moving on to the final component of the Power of GIVE.

The final component in this process is EXPECTATION. If the other components were the package, this last piece is the supersonic delivery jet that will bring it home, completing the cycle and delivering results! How often have you heard people say 'manage your expectations', especially now when it's almost frowned upon to have big dreams and big goals. Not only that, but people have become so disconnected from other human beings that empathy and compassion are becoming non-existent in the daily modus operandi of the socioeconomic culture we live in. Expectation has led people to think of disappointment precisely because of this disconnection, this lack of faith! It is this lack of faith that has lowered our expectations, and opened us up to programming that is driving us to be self-seeking, self-obsessed individuals who are unable to believe without at first seeing.

It's not that you'll believe it when you see it, it's that you'll see it when you believe it.

Expectation is the faith portion of the Power of GIVE, and an essential piece of the process. It can be the most challenging concept to master because you have most likely been programmed to not accept anything that you can't immediately digest through your five basic senses. If you can't see it, hear it, smell it, taste it, or feel it then it's probably not real. On top of that, if it doesn't happen immediately or within a preconceived timeframe, your mind will begin doubting, and you will allow the idea of it not likely happening to permeate until you create enough resistance to give up. This is where most people quit, and the reason why most people will never truly know how close they were to creating magic in their lives. It is the difference between happiness, success, and purpose or just living a default life of mediocrity.

Now let's not confuse this with wishful thinking, because if you skip the previous steps of this formula than you have no package to deliver and, trust me, the plane is not leaving the runway empty! So, you must first create the package and you do that by following the GIVE process in its entirety, taking time to work out all the resistance, reprogramming limiting beliefs, and spending time on understanding it completely. Then you can calmly, intently, from the bottom of your stomach and through your heart expect the outcome to become reality. You can have faith that you will receive exactly what you have requested and worked toward, and your result will be an exact reflection of all the work you have put into this process, as well as the sum of all your thinking during it.

The magic behind Expectation is that if you are not fully aligned, fully committed, fully aware, and fully immersed than you will feel that deep down maybe this won't work, and you're right, it won't. You must feel it in your bones with complete faith in order to become a master of this. But don't despair, because even if you realised that there may have been a small drop of doubt, even if you were not quite convinced, you will still get a result, and that result will be taking you in the right direction. No matter what happens from this point forward, as long as you keep at it you will still always be better, and closer to your goals than ever before. You are no longer operating by default! When this happens, your new-found awareness will highlight to you all the things that may need to be tweaked in order for you to continue down the path — step by step — achieving larger and greater things each time.

I am going to outline what you must do to ensure that you are doing the right type of Expectation thinking. Once you have completed the first three parts of GIVE, you are ready to work on Expectation — thinking as if it is inevitable, as if all that you have worked on is already a reality, and you are in the process of allowing it to show itself. Recall that you learned that with the Time Loop, your results are already real, they have already been created for you, and all you must do now is uncover them. If you maintain your focus, do the exercises a couple of times a day, then all you're left with is inevitability. It will show itself to you. Now it is important that you realise that you will be shown clues that you are on the right path, so be very aware of daily occurrences that align with your goal and say the following sentence when you recognize them:

I am aware, and I was expecting this to happen, I am grateful for being able to witness the alignment of my goals and my reality, because they are already here, and the more I notice the more they appear.

When you begin to see that life begins to happen for you, you will further increase your ability to create using this process and it will ignite a fire in your soul knowing that *you* are making it happen! You will learn more about Expectations and the power of belief in **Principle 11: Faith — You have to believe it to see it!**

Master Training

1. Set your GOAL, based on your desired feelings (self-worth, significance, purpose, etc.). Create a list of Steps — three short-term, three medium, and three long-term. Here are a few examples to help you get started: Increase my business by 25% (med-long term), complete my book (medium), engage in physical activity 3 x week (short), and attain recognition in my field at the award ceremony (long).

2.IMAGINE the possibilities and fantasize about your life having accomplished all your steps. Imagine the feelings that you are receiving.

3.VISUALISE someone who has those things and notice how they behave, feel, act, and what they say. Visualise a day in their life. Visualise yourself being that person, go through a typical day in your mind and realise that this possibility already exists. It is through using the same thoughts, emotions, words, that you noticed in the previous example that will get you there. Reprogram any limiting beliefs that get in the way.

4.EXPECT the results as if they are already here. This type of expectation is a very personal, very quiet internal faith that you feel in your heart, a knowing deep inside your soul that it will be delivered. Notice when you are on the right track and be grateful for its appearance.

PRINCIPLE 5

ALL YOU NEED IS LOVE — UNDERSTANDING BASIC HUMAN NEEDS

There is a plethora of information at your fingertips regarding personality traits, and by doing a simple search, you will discover a marvellous array of systems created to categorise humans into behavioural boxes that pre-determine how they are likely to respond to certain aspects of their life experience. Personality, otherwise known as behavioural traits, have been used to explain why certain people tend to generally behave in a certain manner, and they do this by creating a system of measurement using questions that determine how those people feel and view certain areas of their life. Essentially, these systems are based on the assumption that most human beings are predictable, manageable, and can be easily influenced. If I am able to understand how you are most likely to respond to someone who is dominant and overbearing than I can also use this knowledge to influence you by creating a 'technique' that aligns with those pre-determined behavioural traits. This is not a new thing, and if you just take the time to ponder this you will come to the realisation that all management or leadership books are created to teach one person or group how to effectively manage another person or group using their specific traits and/or needs. This is used in every aspect of life that involves humans managing other humans, and stretches from the workplace to government and everywhere in between. You see, if they can predict how you will behave, then they can sell you anything, and I'm not just referring to things,

I'm talking about selling you 'ideas'.

The beauty of what I am telling you is that you are already very aware of how you, and everyone else on this planet, has become part of a global socio-economic system, a culture, and a group that was programming you from birth to fit in one of these pre-determined boxes. Even the personality you display was created for you. Just take a simple personality test and when you get a result see how neatly you fit into most of the behavioural traits it predicts that you have. It is this that I want you to logically grasp, to understand that all of this is learned behaviour.

All these traits and behaviours are based on what we refer to as human needs. It is these needs, and more specifically the quest for these needs, that determines how we behave in any particular situation. If we have learned to value one need over another, then it is easy to begin creating a behavioural model and fitting people into a personality box. It is also important to understand that throughout our lives, be it through our parents, social groups, or society, we learned ways to satisfy those needs and it is those ways, those methods, that we have learned to create our own behavioural techniques, and our own way of satisfying our needs. These behaviours are predictable, hence the categorisation.

The reason I am telling you this, is because in today's society we have been led to believe that certain people are a certain way and that's why they are more successful, or more determined, or less entrepreneurial, and so on. We have been told that maybe we're just not the type of person for this role, or for this company, and it's because of this belief that we allow ourselves to fit into this personality box. Knowing what you have learned so far in this book, you can now see that this is ridiculous and that you can reprogram your beliefs and your mind to become the type of person you want to be. It's not easy, because this 'system' you have been living under has created a world that is devoted to it. Yet, when you master this manifesto you will no longer live by those rules, you will be able to do anything.

There is a common list of scientifically accepted human needs, and although there may be different names and descriptions for each, they are fundamentally all the same. They all focus on human motivators. The most common or most recognised is Maslow's Hierarchy of Needs, and it is the one theory that you were most likely introduced to during grade school (see diagram). The basic theory consists of five stages beginning with the most basic physiological needs and moving up the scale once each is fulfilled. He later added the innate human need for 'curiosity'. Although this theory receives a lot of criticism from the scientific community because of its simplicity and failure to identify more specific needs based on modern humanity, it is still the rawest, and least influenced by modern socio-economic expectations.

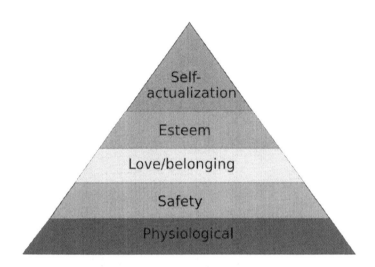

So, in essence, the behavioural box you fit in is how you respond to these basic human needs. However, I am going to show you here which needs you are born with and which ones are learnt, because even this simple breakdown is more complicated and contains aspects that are not innate, but instead are learned, programmed, into the current existential view of life, and can be further dissected to uncover our true nature, giving us the ability to manipulate how we live our lives, and how we feel subjectively. I am going to take you back to the beginning of your physical life, the point when your body was given the power of consciousness, when your higher self, your soul, first entered your physical body for it is here that we can really understand how we formed and inherited our true basic needs. Now, before you begin to question the words you just read, I want you to use what you have learnt thus far and put aside your programmed beliefs about the origins of man and allow me to explain this in a manner that will be acceptable to you. In fact, I am going to show you here how even science must concede to this fact, and it is based on one simple question that science is unable to provide an answer for. That question and the foundation of my list of true innate human needs is this....

What makes you alive?

This is not a question about how to determine if something is living or non-living, that's pretty straightforward to observe, but what science can't explain is what 'sparks' life into something, what makes an assortment of molecules become alive and then show the characteristics that biologists have determined to be those of living things? The truth is this, no one really knows how to explain it in terms of physical reality, yet they all agree that there is an energy or process that is intangible that sparks a thing into life. Now you can call that energy or whatever you like, I have chosen to call it your soul, your being, your higher self, and it is the most powerful reconnection you will make in this lifetime.

So back to where I left off — at some point during the birth process you became alive, you became a conscious being, and the material body that was being made inside your mother's womb received its 'aliveness' or soul. It is at this junction, this coming together of body and soul, where I will demonstrate to you why you are you, and why you have the needs that you have. It is here that we can break down our true essence and understand how all human behaviour is led by these innate needs that we are born with, driving our human experience. These needs are intertwined in your being, sometimes connected, sometimes a struggle, and sometimes in complete misalignment, and my goal is to show you how you can reconnect and engage in a beautiful dance that allows your physical being and your soul to unite, ignite, and fill you with purpose, love, and the power to create an extraordinary life.

We have two very different parts to our being, which also have two very different views of existence. Understanding how they were derived will give you the power to conceptualise which one may be holding a greater dominance over the other, and in most cases, you will find that the physical being is overpowering the soul or spirit and hence driving its own needs above all. The Physical Being is your most recognisable, most prominent being, and consists of all that you identify within this physical reality; it is your ego, your identity, in this world we live in. This ego is you who you think you are, and is the whole of all the programming you received from the day you were conceived until now. It is the part of you that believes in an end and a beginning, it is the one that fears death, that fears loss, because it has no previous existence prior to conception and will have no future existence after your physical death. Its time is limited, and its needs are based on this mortality. It is the gift of physical experience that it holds most sacred and the reason why humanity has struggled with the 'existential crisis' from the start.

Before we continue, you can clearly see that this manifesto has been teaching you to rewrite your beliefs and choose the ones that will empower you to live a purposeful life, a life that you are in control of. It is this Physical Being that I have been teaching you to manipulate so that you can mould and create the life you desire, choosing which beliefs serve you and which ones don't, essentially giving you the true power of free will, the true power of an extraordinary life. All that you have learned thus far about the mind and how to remove and create programs, how to manipulate your physical being in order to take back control of how you experience this life, how to become aware and discover your weaknesses, all this power over your ego, over your physical being allows you to re-connect with your soul, with your higher self and ultimately be in complete alignment in this life. You will now be able to draw on your soul and begin to fuel that spark, slowly growing in intensity, eventually becoming a raging fire, making you a complete, self-actualising, connected, master of the fucking universe.

Now, let's use our power of imagination to understand the process of the soul and physical being becoming one integrated being, and create a story in your mind that will allow you to logically comprehend how I discovered these true basic human needs. By going through this thought process with me, you will be able to more easily assimilate this belief into your subconscious and fully understand how these needs have been driving all human behaviour since the dawn of time.
The story begins with a soul, a spirit, a small part of the magical source of all life. It is boundless and connected to all things, and although we describe it as a single entity, it is one and the same with the source, always connected and always in tune with its existence. It does not comprehend individualism or separation as it is unable to fathom what we physical beings refer to as 'self', its world is energy and eternity and it lives in a state of vibration, it is the god, it is it, it is love!

This source exists in another dimension if you will, another world, yet it is very aware of the physical world in which we live. So, source created a game, a way of experiencing a different way of being. It created a link to this world so that souls could experience what it would be like to live in a physical form, forgetting their connection to their current state of being. When the game began, souls realised how incredible it was to experience a physical form and there were so many possibilities and stories that they could live out during their short time on the playing field. Here on earth, in our dimension, they were overwhelmed at how things feel and taste, how they suffer emotions, and even how they began to fear death during their time playing. Because they chose to forget their power and connection while they played they were unable to remember who they were, and so the objective of the game became to try and discover that connection and reclaim their power inside the game before it ended. These souls quickly began to realise that while they were in the game, they felt disconnected and always like something was missing. They knew deep down that they were part of something greater, but they struggled with the void of knowing their true essence.

The game was difficult, and more and more souls became lost in their physical form, choosing the pleasures of the experience because they could not remember their true nature. It was only when they returned that they realised how poorly they played. They were then able to see just how magical the experience was and how they should have enjoyed being alive in that world. How they should have lived every moment, tasted every food, loved every person, smelled every flower, but they didn't complete the objective, and so they didn't live a physical life with the same love and bliss that they regained by returning to the source.

Now, I want you to pretend that you are one of these souls and you are entering the game, entering a physical being for the first time. The closest I can come to explain the sensation that they must be experiencing is that of you going to sleep and waking up in a dream, unaware of who you are and where you are, with no knowledge of how you got there. It is exhilarating and confusing at the same time and immediately you are blasted with the incredible experience of touch, sound, and an explosion of sensations that you have never experienced before. You notice thought for the first time and it's a wonderful confusing tickling sensation inside your head that brings an emotional flood of energy into your heart and you begin to cry —

you are lost, confused, but somehow delighted with it all!

You have entered the game, and although in the beginning you are still able to comprehend that you are not of this world and that you have chosen to be here, this knowledge begins to blur as the sensations and curiosity of your new reality begin to distract you and pull you toward the novelty of the experience. You begin to forget where you came from, but in your new body, in your new avatar, you feel the connection still in your heart, and it gives you comfort and peace, however, you find that your consciousness is now being affected and you begin to think outside your self. You find a new voice and that voice becomes stronger and more dominant, creating emotions and feeling you have never felt before. You are now a human being!

Please understand that this thought experiment is designed to assist you in making profound changes in your life and whatever you're comfortable with will determine how you should view this scenario. See it as a fable, a legend, a fact, a moral story, a prophecy — anything you want it to be, but no matter what you decide to tell your mind, you can be sure that no other theory or story, be it from school or from science is more accurate than this one. In fact, no one really knows the truth, and there is no hard evidence, if you will, except what you decide to believe — what you decide to accept as programming. In fact, in the next few pages, I will show you how the needs created by this joining of energies, this birth into the material reality I mentioned above, can be used to decipher all human behaviour making it just as 'real' as any other theory of life.

As a human being, you are made up of two parts — a physical being and a soul, or higher self, being creating a unique blend of needs that drives all human behaviour.

First, there is the need for Safety/Security, which is a purely physical being need and is driven by the new-found mortality of the physical body. It is the survival instinct created by being alive in a mortal skin and includes everything from food and shelter to fight and flight, and anything that would jeopardise the physical survival of your human body. How you attain this need will be based on the input from your environment and your programming from the point of your conception.

The second need is the need for Pleasure, as a physical being you are blessed with sensory organs that are naturally seeking stimulation and require input from the physical world. This includes novelty, curiosity, and sexuality. Again, pleasure can be attained through a variety of methods and will be defined by the programming your mind receives. This need is so powerful that it can supersede the need for safety. This need is the one that can create addictive behaviour when the other needs we will discuss are not being met. It drives your being into a lust for euphoria and instant gratification. Unlike other models that tend to associate addictive behaviour with the meeting of several needs, I propose the opposite, that it is the lack of other needs that makes one completely subservient to this purely physical desire. Without satisfying the higher self/soul needs you become a victim to your ego and you distance yourself from your true power. Finally, there is the Human Connection Need that is created from the physical connection that your body experiences during your time in your mother's womb. Since you were born from the body of another your physical being will always crave that connection to another human being. From the time you are born, your physical being develops a tie to other physical beings which manifests into a variety of feelings and emotions. It is where the desire for significance arises, and although we will discuss significance further in the soul needs, this physical significance is where the rise of jealousy and competition occurs, and causes humans to want to be more, and feel more important, than their counterparts. This is not to be confused with self-worth, but instead, it is an existential selfishness born out of the basic and natural need for physical connection. If you think about the animal world it is the raw desire to be the leader of the pack, and will drive an animal to even kill family to obtain status and significance. You must understand that although I am showing that these needs alone are more animalistic and almost inhuman, they are a natural part of what being a complete human being is all about. Alone, they can create psychopaths, but when combined with the higher needs of the soul, they will produce powerful, fully empowered, well-balanced human beings. This is how we become great, this is how we discover our power and live a truly happy and fulfilled physical life.

Now we move onto the needs of the soul, the spirit, the higher self, and again I implore you to contemplate this possibility with an open mind — after all, it is an open mind that will allow you to change your life, and more importantly an open heart.
Your soul is made of pure energy and, as we discussed earlier, becomes joined with your physical being to create you. Although it has the pleasure

of experiencing the physical dimension and all its wonderful sensory pleasures, it or YOU immediately feel that your connection to the source is diminished and hence the first need of your soul is created — the need for spiritual connection. Your soul wants to connect to its true origin, and is always seeking to find that connection to that pure energy and unconditional love. It has no hidden agenda except this one simple basic need, to connect with the source and allow his/her physical expression to be in touch with the power that it was once a part of, this power is pure LOVE. This need is essential to keep your being alive and aligned — it is what you are, and without it, you lose your humanity, like the serial killer whose straight face and cold empty eyes, have no visual signs of compassion. A cold heart and an empty soul. This can explain why just the thought of someone so callous and cold brings a million shivers down your spine. It is complete disconnection and you can't even fathom how a human being could possibly be driven to such deeds because you are still connected, still a whole.

On the other hand, complete submission to this need, to this spiritual bliss, is also not the ideal path and although today's society is very well anchored closer to the negative end, being completely devoted to this without acknowledging the beauty of physicality is denying your true self. You are all of you, and although the physical needs alone will drive you into torment, the only time you will experience pure love is when you move onto the next phase and depart your physical experience. So, what I am saying to you is that a strong connection to this inner authentic YOU will create a life that is aligned, magical, and fulfilling!

You see, the soul wants to reconnect, and it wants to show you that you are it, that you are part of the whole, the source, god — whatever you want to label it, and not just the egocentric bag of skin you occupy. It wants to give you the gift of knowing so that you can create a life that is an adventure, exciting, and purposeful, fully enjoying your physicality and being able to create and manifest like a god. This soul mission creates the profound need to find purpose in your life, it is here that fulfillment arises, and true happiness is created. This need leads to constant growth, the search for passion and purpose, a quest that is never truly achieved, but instead becomes a way of living.

Carl Jung the great psychiatrist and brilliant mind highlighted the 'spiritual problem' of our time, and he explains how the loss of our connection has created the society we live in today. A society that is lost, insignificant, and impotent.

"Small and hidden is the door that leads inward, and the entrance is barred by countless prejudices, mistaken assumptions, and fears. Always one wishes to hear of grand political and economic schemes, the very things that have landed every nation in a morass. Therefore, it sounds grotesque when anyone speaks of hidden doors, dreams, and a world within. What has this vapid idealism got to do with gigantic economic programmes, with the so-called problems of reality?

But I speak not to nations, only to the individual few, for whom it goes without saying that cultural values do not drop down like manna from heaven, but are created by the hands of individuals. If things go wrong in the world, this is because something is wrong with the individual, because something is wrong with me. Therefore, if I am sensible, I shall put myself right first. For this I need — because outside authority no longer means anything to me — a knowledge of the innermost foundations of my being, in order that I may base myself firmly on the eternal facts of the human psyche."

—Carl Jung, The Meaning of Psychology for Modern Man

<u>Physical/Ego Being Needs</u>
Safety / Security
Physical Bonding/Connection
Pleasure/Novelty
<u>Soul/Spiritual Being Needs</u>
Love
<u>Joint Need</u>
Purpose

As I mentioned before, these needs are entangled and form what I call 'Whole Needs', and each one is vitally important to your wellbeing and the wellbeing of humanity. Knowing and understanding these needs, and their relationship to each other, allows you to observe your own behaviour, your own ideals and beliefs, your feelings, and enable you to refocus your life so that you are completely aligned and able to truly live life unlimited. Now, although each need is important, some needs can be 'inflamed' more easily than others, creating a tilt in how you view and live your life. This has been known for centuries, and today the manipulation of your needs occurs immediately after birth and carries on throughout your life, making you heavily focused on the ego needs in order to satisfy the current socio-economic model of consumerism and scientism while ignoring the soul/spiritual and joint needs.

Soul Needs

Having your soul needs met will automatically ensure that your other needs are being met in healthy ways. In this sense, you are connected, aligned, and your soul begins to spark your whole being into a powerful creator. I have illustrated this below, in simple terms, using a scale of 0 to 2, 0 being when your needs are never met, 1 when they are met sometimes, and 2 when they are always met.

<u>Physical/Ego Being Needs</u>
Safety / Security — **2**
Physical Bonding/Connection — **2**
Pleasure/Novelty — **2**

<u>Soul/Spiritual Needs</u>
Love — **2**

<u>Joint Need</u>
Purpose — **2**

Addict needs

The Addict has his/her needs completely out of alignment, has been consumed by the need for pleasure, and is no longer getting the other required needs. Although they are still able to meet some of them, even minimally, it is very difficult to stop the behaviour unless there is a rebalancing. Any time a rebalancing is required, focusing on the spiritual needs, along with providing the safety and connection from other humans, will begin to shift the need for pleasure to a safer, more positive place. Pleasure seeking is a very disconnected state and is such a potent physical need that it will trump even the basics, such as the need for safety and survival. Another example of human behaviour gone astray is if we were to satisfy the need for physical bonding and connection and leave all else the same. We would then get a person that seeks pleasure using others as a source, a need for significance through hedonistic means results in sadism. See the Addict needs score below.

<u>Physical/Ego Being Needs</u>
Safety / Security — **0**
Physical Bonding/Connection — **1**
Pleasure/Novelty — **2**

<u>Soul/Spiritual Needs</u>
Love — **0**

<u>Joint Need</u>
Purpose — **0**

Current societal needs

When the soul or spiritual needs are ignored, a dangerous physical needs focus is created, pleasure-seeking ensues, and insecurity and insignificance rises, making people lust for power and significance through the means thrust down their throats on a daily basis — consumerism. There is a disconnection, people feel lost, and they search out means of pleasure that are disempowering and soul destroying. The human being and their 'whole needs' are essential to understanding the larger connection of our existence, and it's this connection that we begin to feel and see every day that removes the need for a beginning or an end. It is the sun shining over the ocean and kissing the waves with its light, the magnificent tree dancing in the wind, or the simple touch of someone we love — all of this becomes part of who we are, and when we know that we are a part of it, the fear of what was and what is to come disappears like the night at the break of day. We are freed of the existential crisis that modern society has created, and we feel boundless, powerful, and our soul is lit — glowing like the midday sun! See the Societal needs score below.

<u>Physical/Ego being needs</u>
Safety / Security — **1**
Physical Bonding/Connection — **1**
Pleasure/Novelty — **2**

<u>Soul/spiritual needs</u>
Love — **0-1**

<u>Joint Need</u>
Purpose — **0**

<u>Master Training</u>

Contemplate your own life and how you feel about yourself at home, work, and play.

How are you meeting these basic 'Whole Needs'?

Are there needs that you are not meeting regularly in healthy ways?

If you had a clear purpose and felt connected would you feel insecure at work or in business?

If your safety and security are threatened, would it be difficult to love and find purpose?

When someone is lonely and distant from others how could they be compensating for the lack of their physical bonding need?

What type of person might you become if your soul needs are not being met?

How does someone meet the need for significance if they are not satisfying it through purpose?

What feelings are you searching for?

What needs will these feelings meet?

How else can you meet those needs and in turn get the desired feeling?

PRINCIPLE 6

ABRACADABRA — THE MAGIC OF WORDS

When was the last time you heard that word 'abracadabra'? Probably not for a very long time, and most likely not since you were a child watching Saturday morning cartoons after eagerly awaking at the crack of dawn to catch all the best ones. This single word was usually the prelude to some pretty amazing feats of magic and wonder that tickled your senses and charmed your innocent and captive mind! Just the sound of the word itself immediately triggered a euphoric reaction in your body, causing your heart to beat faster than before, and your hair to stand on end from the surge of electrified anticipation of wonder to come. It was automatic, instantaneous, and predictable! Abracadabra meant wonder, magic, miracles, and just like all things adult, you allowed that word to remain a child word and now, in your adult life, probably don't even like the sound of it anymore.

Why did it lose its lustre?

Based on the information you've learned thus far in this manifesto, you can easily see that the beliefs and ideas that you adopted were focused on your 'reality' and the word 'abracadabra' subconsciously brings feelings of disappointment and anger because in your new reality the miracle of magic is almost completely gone.

First, let's look at what 'abracadabra' really means, and why it was used in magic. You've probably never wondered what the word actually meant, or if it even had a definition. Until this instant you just thought of it as a peculiar word, a word made up to entice children into the fantastical world of magic. And, while part of that is true, there is a deeper meaning, a historical definition that I will share with you here, that if you had known might have led you to hold onto the word into your adulthood, into your acceptable reality. And maybe, that's why it is used less and less because a word like this can awaken your childhood curiosity and give you the power to create your own magic.

The first known mention of the word was in a book called *Liber Medicinalis* in the third century AD by Quintus Serenus Sammonicus, a physician to the Roman emperor Caracalla. It was in this book that he prescribed its use to defeat disease and misfortune by having sufferers wear an amulet containing the word written in the form of a triangle or 'abracabrangle'. The word was said to contain great power and have healing properties throughout its history. In fact, silver and gold talismans have been discovered with the word inscribed on them dating as far back as the 6th century, proving that this powerful word was much more than what it has become today. So, when I give you its English translation and meaning, it will all make sense to you why this word, this power has been dumbed down for you, and has been turned into child's play. The word translates into "I create as I speak" and was considered a magical formula from the divine. In essence, your words create your reality! Abracadabra!

This principle will help you to understand the power that words have on our reality and how speaking or thinking with these words essentially creates the type of life you experience. This has been known for thousands of years and, yet no form of education has ever been designed to give you the ability to use this to help you — in fact, most curriculums regardless of their academic placement use words to create boundaries and limitations in your vocabulary so that you stay within the parameters set out by those who created them. The truth is even far stranger and far more deliberate than you could have ever imagined, and language itself has been labeled and organised into such a way that what you believe is that 'proper' English, or French, or any nationalistic language for that matter, is only proper because it was taught to you that way. The Institute Professor Emeritus at the Massachusetts Institute of Technology (MIT) and laureate professor at the University of Arizona, Noam Chomsky — considered to be the father of modern linguistics — states that the language for communication created and taught in schools is not natural language but one specifically created to bind a society together. To induce nationalistic identity and ultimately a sense of distinctiveness, not just between countries but also within itself, leading to ingroups and outgroups as defined by the vernacular they use regularly. In layman's terms, the way people speak in low income, low educated neighbourhoods versus those who speak 'proper' English.

What I want you to understand is that the words that our schools, our government, our media, our colleagues, and our family use have a profound effect on how you think and feel about life. The words that you learn, and then use to speak and think with, are moulding your reality. Your vernacular creates your visual representation of the world, and the language you think with essentially creates your experienced reality. So, in order to create the life you have always dreamt of, you will need to use this knowledge not only to reassess the words you use, but also understand how words are used to manipulate your thoughts and your decisions. I will show you how to walk confidently through this minefield of word bombs, and give you the tools to disarm them. I will also show you how you can rearrange your vocabulary to give you even more power in how your life unfolds.

Now, I want you to ponder something before we carry on. Like everything in this manifesto, it is up to you to open your mind and at least become aware of the possibility that you are greater and more powerful than you ever imagined, and with this knowledge you can truly become the master of your fate. I say this because all it takes is the correct placement of a few words to destroy your desire to take on critical thinking and actively create the life you desire. This manifesto is not for everyone, and unfortunately, it is those that are living life on terms not their own that will oppose and ignore the message in these pages. Your freedom, your magic, your life, will come under fire, and maybe even be condemned by those closest to you. Programming is a powerful tool and there are words that have been created and used to prevent you from discovering your power and igniting your soul. You will know these words and you will have feelings about them, yet now you will understand why they conjure those emotions and how to effectively prevent them from sabotaging your growth.

Let's discuss some common words that have had a profound impact on who you are today, and how their use and their generally accepted meaning creates your reality.

Science

The word 'science' immediately makes something true or factual, based on the belief that someone who is highly educated has proved it through some form of test or mathematical theory. It is an absolute, uncontestable, and allows people to win arguments based on proof that very few understand how to replicate. This word and subject has been indoctrinated into young minds for a few generations and is now the defining belief in modern socio-economic culture. It is so powerful, that very few dare to challenge its grasp on today's reality. The truth, however, is that the word has removed the ability to discuss or even offer different yet feasible interpretations which scientists have deemed irrelevant. People are discouraged from challenging theories and laws, even though those 'laws' are based on pre-defined parameters that were created to fit the desired outcome. Most laws are dependent on theoretical interpretations — the law of gravity is based on an assumption and uses various generally accepted formulas which were engineered to fit the equations. My point is not to challenge science itself, but instead to allow you to at least consider that what you believe to be fact, is based on someone else's interpretation and on a textbook that was written and regurgitated to you in school. Science is a belief, yet it has penetrated mass society. It has definitely enriched our lives, yet it has also made the fool believe he is intelligent.

Conspiracy

This word is used to label a point of view that does not fit in with the approved or accepted version of reality. People who believe in conspiracies are usually outcasts and criticized. Add 'theory' to the end of this word and you got the making of some 'wack job' views of accepted reality. When someone mentions a conspiracy theory, it usually means that they are oblivious to 'science' and should really be more 'educated'. It is usually accompanied by laughter, ridicule, and annihilating the conspiracy theorist's point of view to worthless conversation ashes. This is the mass definition and feeling of the word, yet before it was used in popular culture there was another term used to describe this type of viewpoint. It was called critical thinking, and it was the ability to view situations with an open mind, free of limitations and generally accepted mass beliefs. If you want to truly take back your path in life and truly find your power, then you will need to be able to listen to all viewpoints and consider them without condemning and without judgement.

Education

This word represents something that should be available to all and is of utmost importance in the formation of young people to ensure they are able to successfully join the workforce and be well compensated for their knowledge. Most believe that education is a right, is the key to the future, and is perceived as a foundation for intelligence and success. It is generally accepted that everyone should be educated, and that we have the responsibility to educate those who are less fortunate around the world. Now once again, I am going to challenge your beliefs and ideals because as you know, education (as we know it) is a fairly modern system created around the dawn of mass cities and nationalistic societies. It was a perfect way to mobilise a workforce by ensuring they had the skills and mental programming to perform the tasks required whilst being manageable. Education was a form of indoctrination created so that the masses would understand how to behave and how to accept and listen to authority as defined by the education system. It creates law-abiding, authority accepting, money driven, conforming citizens that lack critical thinking and creativity. In fact, ADHD is the label created for such creative, un-conforming minds, leaving the rest to become highly educated, yet less intelligent and completely immersed in the dogma of their education. Education does not equal intelligence. On the contrary, those with minimal post-secondary education, those that were the rebels and free thinkers, are the ones who own businesses and have the creative capacity to create lives that are enriching. Those that don't use their creative minds are run into the corners of society with mental health issues, squashed down into medical diagnoses that dampen their minds and their spirits.

Government

The word 'government' represents an organisation that is appointed by the people to run the affairs of the community. Many blame the government for economic and societal woes, yet they believe that somehow one party is more capable than another. We also feel that all politicians are somewhat corrupt, however, we choose to accept this and allow the system to be what it is. The truth is, no matter what party is in power, no matter what the campaign entails, the government is just a cog in the system that effectively manages the world's economy. When you complain about taxes, debt, or deficit, you're essentially just spitting in the ocean, as it is the inner working of the system that drives the process. Every government has parameters that are instilled in its very nature and all parties must operate within them. Most issues that are tackled or highlighted during campaigning are insignificant in the larger picture, however, most people feel that it is these issues that will change society and they get behind the nominee, joining groups and rallying for decisions that will never change the fundamental system that runs the socio-economic machine.

DNA

The building blocks of life made up of a type of protein strand, 'DNA' is what people believe is the reason for hereditary disease and also some personality traits that are passed on from our parents. It is science, and therefore a sacred cow when it comes to defining human beings. It has been used to incite the acceptance of cancer and other diseases being hereditary, ensuring that you believe your sickness came from your parents and not the current environmental and societal poisons. It is part of the pharmaceutical conditioning that medicine (drugs) is the only way to remain healthy. There is enough research to confirm that it is your environment, your mind, and ultimately your programmed beliefs that determine your overall health and wellbeing. This you must understand is part of the secret that will liberate you, allowing you to effectively manage your health without over prescription and without fear.

Fake news

A relatively new term, 'fake news' has been created to identify what is acceptable and true. It is perceived as a problem and needs to be eliminated in order to protect people's views of reality. It has so much support that entire nations are allowing the most powerful companies on the internet to decide what is fake and what is not. This is potentially one of the greatest coups in modern times, yet most people are too concerned with the fear of terrorists, the Kardashians, the newest iPhone, the government spending, etc. that they are oblivious to laws that are being passed in plain sight which will give these companies the ability to censor at their discretion. The bigger problem here is that most people are unable to decipher what they should or should not believe, and have become defenders of this process, allowing the manipulation of the only true free form of unbiased information available to the masses — the internet. I urge you to ask questions and never assume that what you are being told is the truth.

Terrorism

The word 'terrorism' is used regularly by media and pop culture and is now engrained in our language. It brings up feelings of fear and anger and is perceived to identify those of the Muslim religion who are evil. This word, and its various depictions, are responsible for an entire shift in mass perception. It is propaganda on the largest scale and has allowed the invasion of entire countries to happen with the unwitting approval of 'educated' societies. It has created an enemy and a biased view of an entire religion, but much worse, it has created a reason, a movement in its own right — radicalisation and terror groups are a result of it; they are not the cause. Put that in your mind and let it sink in! Once you understand that what I am teaching you here has been used and has been known to those who are currently pulling the strings, you will no longer be influenced by it. Your freedom, your ability to create change in your life depends on understanding what is happening around you so that you are in control of your life.

Mental Health

A relatively new term that highlights the suffering that many people endure due to mental issues, 'mental health' is perceived not as a positive 'health' but rather a depressed mind that is in need of support and empathy. This has encouraged the overdiagnosis of mental issues creating an epidemic in the western world. It drives the belief that if you are currently confused and unable to conform to society's perceived notion of a healthy mind, you probably have a condition. It satisfies the need to belong by blaming your state of mind on some sort of inherent 'condition' that you are not in control of, and creates an identity with 'mental health' as the root cause. Instead, the fact is that having those types of thoughts and feelings are normal and can most likely be resolved by understanding the reasons behind them — such us our human needs, our beliefs, our desire to fit in — and then knowing that it is simply a facet of the mind that is out of alignment with our true nature. Now, I'm not saying that there are situations where this is not the case, but what I am proposing is that by labelling it, and medicating it, you are essentially encouraging its very existence. Most cases of mental health issues appear in those that are outliers, and non-conformists, those that feel that something is not quite right with their reality. I hope this manifesto, this guide will allow you to see that you are right, that there is something out of alignment and learning these skills will give you the power to understand why, and how to create a life that you can live with.

This was just a taste of the wonderful magic of words and how their meaning and their use can create deep-rooted beliefs and define your reality. The language you speak is loaded with words and phrases that are defining your identity and your reality at this precise moment. Taking the time to contemplate this will open your eyes to how effective language has become at defining your society.

Now, I want you to visit the language that you use on a daily bases, especially the repetitive words and phrases that you use to communicate your experience, and see how they determine what you have been creating in your reality. This is an important part of self-awareness and it is the language you use that subconsciously sabotages your life success. It is the common things you say and think that define your results in life. A poor language results in a poor life, and I'm not talking about what you would call 'proper' language, I'm talking about using words and phrases that subconsciously create limiting beliefs, stifling your ability to discover your true potential. Let's look at a few common phrases that are popular yet catastrophic in terms of their negative effect on your life.

"Why does this always happen to me?"
"I'm not educated enough to get that job."
"I always screw up my relationships."
"There are no good guys/girls left out there for me."
"I don't have the time."
"Money is the root of all evil."
"Life's a bitch."
"I have to grind to make it."
"My metabolism is slow."
"People are rude."
"I have no luck."
"I can't afford it."
"The economy is ruining my business."
"I hate my life."

There are too many to list, but I'm sure you get the picture. Everyone has certain phrases and words they use that have become like an automated response to certain events or situations, and it is these 'automatic' thoughts or words that cripple your mind, and ultimately your success.

Let's use the "my metabolism is slow" phrase as an example because it encompasses so many things that we have discussed thus far in this manifesto, and one that I came across regularly with my weight loss clients. Now, you must remember one thing, most of my clients have never been diagnosed with any type of metabolic issues. Those that have been able to successfully change the language they used and, by following the steps in this manifesto, were able to lose weight and keep it off! A slow metabolism is usually a *result* of excessive fat and weight, not the *cause* of being overweight.

"Slow metabolism is the direct result of excessive fat and weight, not the cause of being overweight! It's science!"

By simply changing the words we use, we can alter the programming in our subconscious mind allowing us to insert instructions that are in-line with our desires. This is one strategy that we discuss in reprogramming the mind and is vital if you are going to speak to yourself using the right language. If you continually speak the types of words and phrases that are absolute and negative in nature, then by default you will sow those seeds into your reality and it will reflect your words precisely. Just think about the two people at the beginning of this manifesto and think about how their words, their thinking, their beliefs created their life — it all started with words! Change your most common negative words and begin to see the fruits of your labor. Instead of "life's a bitch" say "life is an adventure." Instead of "I'm so unlucky" say "what am I being taught here". Instead of "I have no connections" say "I only need the one right connection." Bam! Magic starts to happen.

Master Training

Write down a list of words and phrases that you regularly use that are taking away your power and sabotaging your success.

How could you rephrase or use different words that would change how you feel about a situation?

What need is your subconscious meeting by using these words?

How could you satisfy those needs and still use the right type of language?

PRINCIPLE 7

THE RIGHT STUFF — REMOVING LIMITING BELIEFS AND REPROGRAMMING THE MIND-BODY

To have 'the right stuff' is much more complicated than just possessing a short list of skills and attributes that would make you perfect for a specific type of outcome. You have already learned that first, you must identify what it is you want to achieve, what goals you are truly desiring before you can start putting together a list of what 'the right stuff' really looks like for you. And then, once you have used the Power of GIVE, self-awareness, needs analysis, and the knowledge of the mind and body, you can really begin to build 'the right stuff' and remove the 'wrong stuff'!

This principle of the manifesto will give you the practical knowledge and tools to mould and create the type of behaviours and thoughts that align with your greatest desires using the principles you have already learnt thus far. In most cases, and in most self-development guides, you are given this part of the toolbox without the foundational information and knowledge needed and as a result, this step is just simply ineffective. So, please make sure you have fully read and understood all the previous principles so that you may make the most out of this section.

(Note: You can always take the online course that accompanies this manifesto so that you are a master of each principle before moving on to the next. It is free with this book and available at your fingertips whenever you need to access this powerful information.)

The first thing I want to address is: what exactly is a limiting belief? If you have been following along, you will easily be able to pinpoint which beliefs are working for you and which ones need to be annihilated. The only way to truly identify them is to first use the Power of GIVE, and specifically the visualisation techniques that we practiced. Once you have a desire or want, visualising yourself having achieved it will bring up a feeling of resistance, or rather a thought in the back of your mind which doesn't quite believe that you can get what you're asking for. Using your self-awareness, you can capture these thoughts and decipher them into a belief that is essentially sabotaging your desire. It is these beliefs that we will restructure or remove so that you can be totally aligned and set your soul on fire, making anything that you wish a reality.

Let me share a personal story with you that highlights the control that these limiting beliefs may have on you. When I was young, my parents immigrated to Canada from Portugal to seek out a new adventure and a better life. My father was a welder and had worked in the shipyards in our small city since he was 12 years old (yes that's right, that's the way it was in those days). Every penny he earned went back to his mom and dad to help support the family. But it was not just his good nature that compelled him to give up his money, it was his mom who demanded and enforced it. There was no pity or shame, it was simply the way you ran family affairs in the lower class of the then fascist dictatorship. My father became a good welder, and his work ethic and toughness earned a few raises throughout his first five years, moving him from making just a few cents a day to almost a dollar when he was 17. He kept a few of these pay increases secret so that he would have a little cash to go out and have a beer with his friends, but his guilt and loyal nature always led him to give most of it up to help with his three younger brothers who only had one pair of shoes each. When he was 18, his brothers and his parents were now able to support themselves without having to take all that he was earning. He continued to climb the ladder, and by 20 was one of the few on the block who had a motorcycle and could afford good clothes —not expensive clothes — but he was better off than most of the other young men of poor families that lived in their neighbourhood.

Somewhere along the way, my father became a good man, and although I am familiar with his story I don't *really* know what experiences and what programming created his belief system and eventually moulded his life. I do believe that being brought up in a place where a fascist government, and those connected to it, were the ones that had it all made him empathise with a more socialist, if not communist, idea of society. What I can attest to, is that my father is incorruptible, and his loyalty and honesty are so righteous that despite my biases, I have never met a more genuine, unshakably honest, kind-hearted human being. He is this to his core. His experience of life has definitely programmed many of my current beliefs, which I have embraced. But, there is another set of beliefs and programs that I have chosen to reprogram, and it is these beliefs that my father was unable to readjust in his own life. These beliefs are: money is the root of evil and greed, ambition is filled with lies and cheaters, and Jesus himself was a poor man. My father developed a belief that is actually quite common among his generation in Portugal, the idea that there is nobility in being poor. This programmed belief was passed on to me at an early age, and not because my father didn't want me to be rich or successful, he always encouraged me to be a good student and get a good job, but it was the 'in between the lines' programming that was far more powerful. The passing comments of 'they have all that money because they're crooks' or 'those rich don't care about the workers' or ' when you have too much money you become greedy and forget the rest', were just some of the phrases that he made to others, to my mom, or at the TV. As a young child, this material began to sink into my subconscious mind, like a small creek slowly carving a valley out of a mountain, the beliefs began to run deep. My father has now lived in Canada for 37 years and he has 'enough', as he would put it, to ensure that he can live comfortably, take holidays to Portugal every year, and live his retirement worry free. He *could* have been very well off in terms of money and assets, however, he shunned away from buying rental properties, or investing in opportunities that made many of his friends here in Canada much wealthier than he is. This led to more than a few arguments between him and my mom, as she was always inclined to buy an investment property and take more risks, but my dad would always have the last say and it was always one of caution and stability. My dad was afraid to risk what he had worked so hard to earn and his beliefs created his life. Now, I do have to clarify that I am not condoning my father's decisions, he worked very hard all of his life and he was and is an amazing father and friend, what I am showing you here is that he could have been both, it was only his beliefs that prevented it. And it is not my place to judge his idea of a good life, his experiences moulded his mind and he was living a life in complete alignment with those beliefs.

I can look at my father's life and make some assumptions on how he developed these beliefs, but despite having been a part of his life for 43 years and the closest person to observing his life other than my mom, I cannot claim to know what my father's subjective experience truly was. I will never know what he really thinks or feels subjectively, but I will make an attempt so that we can see how these beliefs were created and more specifically how my own limiting beliefs developed.

By understanding his past I can guess that my father's fear of risk developed directly from the responsibility of having to provide for his younger siblings and the household in general. He never learned to be entrepreneurial because it wasn't even a thing during those fascist times. He knew that he had a duty, and he knew that he could have *some* things, but he was obligated to be responsible when it came to money. There were no rich or successful people in his circle, they were always the 'elite', those other people born with silver spoons in their mouths, the royalty. This developed into a powerful belief, and it moulded his character creating pride in being an honest, responsible worker. My dad actually told me once that when he was born he was stamped on the back with the word 'worker' and that is what he would be until he died. It would drive all his decisions around money and risk-taking, leading only to very safe, very honest investments that would not threaten his stability in any way.

This leads us to my life and how I developed a similar limiting belief around money, yet it took a very different shape for me. I become a rogue, a risk taker, and a free spirit. By the time I was 21 and had done the college thing, I wanted risk and excitement and so essentially went against the grain, leaving education behind, to go out and have adventure and become an entrepreneur. I believed that I would be rich one day! I wanted to be 'somebody' and have the 'worker' stamp washed off of my back.
So I did exactly that.

By 19 I had opened an event company and by 24 my first nightclub. I thought I was going to make it big, I was going to show my dad that I could have it all. The only problem was that I had never dealt with my limiting belief and, trust me, it was there the whole time, hanging in the background like a shadow, sabotaging my every move. I blew most of the money I made — and I made a lot — making bad investments in one failed business after another. I began to believe that I was not good enough or not part of the 'in' group that were making big moves and living the life. I began to listen to the voice inside that I was never going to make it, which led me to begin drinking and using drugs only adding to my despair and inability to succeed. At 37, I was broke, divorced, and carrying around some pretty big bags of issues that I never imagined having when I was younger. "I should have saved my money and I should have taken fewer chances and been satisfied with being a 'worker'", was the chatter in my subconscious mind. Until I was able to confront my belief system, I was never going to achieve my financial goals.

This type of retrospection is an important way to understand one's own limiting beliefs and ideals, however, it can only be done once we are able to do it without judgement and without prejudice. You must view your life experience from a bird's eye view, never blaming, never judging — purely to understand the programming that occurred so that you may release any hidden emotional ties and begin the process of reprogramming on purpose. Also, one of the cardinal rules of this process is to make sure you don't develop a sense of responsibility to help those that have beliefs that you may not agree with. No one can be helped if they haven't first sought it themselves.

In order to remove the type of programming that is no longer serving us, we must identify what those programs are. There are two types of limiting beliefs — the ones you can consciously point out through conscious thinking and the ones that remain hidden in your subconscious mind. Obviously, it is the hidden ones that pose the greatest threat to our life success, and it is these that must first be identified so that we can reprogram them to suit our desires. To do this, you must understand the principles that have been laid out in this manifesto, which will assist you in pinpointing them and eventually releasing them from your mind. Using the power of GIVE you can identify the unwanted programs like a doctor uses an ultrasound or scan to find a tumor, and then with the precision of a surgical procedure remove them from your mind. But first, you must have the awareness and understanding that comes with knowing the other principles in this manifesto so that you can identify if it is a dangerous tumor or if it's a necessary component that needs to be left alone.

At this point, you should already know what those unwanted beliefs are, but just to help you verbalise them I am going to highlight some of the most common ones that I have helped clients with over the years. These are common phrases that are loaded with programmed beliefs, causing their thinkers and believers to move away from the very things they wish they could have or be. Deciphering these sentences will allow you to pinpoint what the belief is, where it came from, what needs it satisfies, and why your life is where it is.

Financial

- I don't have enough money to start the business.
- I have no connections that can help me with financing.
- Money doesn't make you happy.
- I can't afford to lose money trying to make my dream come true.
- There's no way I can make that kind of money.

Relationships

- There are no good girls/guys anymore.
- I always meet the worst type of people.
- I'm just not that good-looking.
- I'm too independent to have a partner.

Purpose

- I just don't have time to focus on my hobby.
- I don't have the money to be able to follow my purpose.
- I used to be great at it, but now I have responsibilities.
- It's more important to provide for my family.

Spiritual

- I don't need any help with my issues.
- Meditation and self-awareness are for the weak.
- We're born, we die, the end.
- How could God allow this to happen?

I'm going to select one of the phrases above and take you through a process, in the Master Training below, that will remove the limiting belief and allow you to align your subconscious with the desired outcome of your choice. Like any new skill, it takes some time and practice to become a master at eliminating beliefs that no longer serve you, but once this becomes second nature you will have the ability to create a powerful belief system that will catapult you to success. Like a cat's ability to land on their feet without a slight hesitation, you too will automatically mould your mind, landing a life experience that you have always wanted.

<u>Master Training</u>

Note: I have answered the questions below to give you an example of how to complete this process for your own limiting beliefs.

First, select a phrase or thought to analyze.
"I don't have enough money to start the business."

Then ask yourself, "what is the limiting belief?"
You can't start a business without having a lot of money

Identify the source: Identifying the thought or phrase can be done using the power of GIVE or, if you are already consciously aware, then this process becomes even easier.

> *1.* When did this belief arise? *When I was in high school.*

> *2.* Was there a particular event or events that occurred that caused you to believe this? *My friends always said that it takes money to make money.*

> 3. Is this a conscious thought that you actively have, or is it a deeper subconscious resistance you discovered during your visualisation? *When I visualised myself having the business, I kept having the thought that it's not possible because I don't have the money.*

Eliminate distortion: Programmed beliefs may be deeply entrenched in what we assume is our identity, so much so that we have imagined distorted views of reality to serve those beliefs. This section removes the distorted views and allows a clearer more rational view of those limiting beliefs.

4. Are there people with similar circumstances, or maybe even less favorable ones, that were able to open a business and succeed? *Yes. I'm sure there are.*

5. Is it true that if one person with the same financial situation as you did it, that probably many more have done it too? *Yes, it's true.*

6. If these other people can do it, is it possible that you can also do it? *Yes*

Uncover needs: Our whole needs drive our feelings and our decisions, always leading us toward satisfying those needs in the most efficient and effective manner, which may not be the most congruent way of achieving a successful life. Identifying these needs will allow us to fulfill them by other means more suitable to our desired outcome.

7. What needs are you satisfying by holding on to this belief? *I want to feel <u>connected</u> to my friends, so if I suddenly start making different contacts and spending time doing 'business' things they may not accept me, or they might mock me for trying to change. I am scared to take risks because I may lose my <u>stability</u> in life.*

8. If you were to change your thinking and your beliefs, how else could you satisfy those needs? *I could find even more connection with new types of people that have achieved what I want. I could start slowly and maybe build my business part-time, so I can still feel stable in my life.*

9. What is your ultimate goal in having your own business? What feelings are you after and what needs will this satisfy? *I am tired of working in a job I don't really like. If I could make a living doing what I love, then I would not have to force myself to get*

up every morning. I want to feel great about myself, feel like I'm in control. I want to feel like I have a purpose in my life.

NOTE: I have underlined the needs in the responses so that you can see how to formulate your own responses, asking yourself more and more questions, probing your own thoughts so that you may draw out what it is that you are truly needing in your life. This really ties in with the power of GIVE, and allows you to understand why you have the goals you have and if the 'step' that you're trying to take is actually the right one for you. In this case, maybe opening a business is not necessarily the right path, and discovering other ways to satisfy those needs may uncover other avenues that will be more effective and more congruent with your needs. The need for stability is what is causing the resistance to change, as well as the societal connection to friends and family. It trumps the need for purpose because although in this case, the person is after a greater connection and more purpose, the need is still being met by their 'responsibility' to their current identity; although in a very small amount, which makes it very difficult to change.

Create alternative aligned beliefs: We now are ready to create new beliefs that align with our desires and we do this by creating a phrase that can substitute the old limiting belief. Keep in mind the needs that we uncovered to ensure we still maintain them, but now in a more positive manner. In this instance, we need to ensure that our phrase gives us stability and societal connection.

> *10.* What belief do I want to have that will empower me and be aligned with my needs? *Many successful entrepreneurs started their businesses on their kitchen table and came from neighbourhoods just like mine. Many financially successful business owners that had little money got huge investments after they started with a small business by themselves.*

NOTE: The questions above are to be used as a guide so that you may find the necessary information to give you the power to change your beliefs. You can create your own questions by understanding what it is that you are trying to discover. This type of self-probing is a skill that will bring you tremendous power in all areas of your life and allow you to change beliefs and thoughts to suit your life without guilt, shame, or judgement.

Create the Memory: This is the key part of reprogramming the subconscious mind. Where there was once a limiting belief based on a memory, there will now be a congruent, aligned, manufactured memory that will be considered to be true by your mind. The subconscious makes no distinction between a real memory or an imagined one, because in actuality there is no difference — both are just facets of the mind and only exist in your thoughts. The 'real' event in the past no longer exists, how you now perceive it in the present is what is 'real' to you. This is powerful stuff and has been known to psychologists and neuroscientists for years. False memories can be a crippling master when they are based around a previous trauma or event, however, knowing this, and using it to your benefit allows you to rewire any past trauma or event to relieve pain and create empowering beliefs.

- From the **identify the source** section above, use your imagination to view the initial 'event' that caused the limiting belief from a third-person perspective. Go back in time and watch yourself, be like a movie camera or drone hovering over your past self, watching and listening to the entire event. Notice the details that you may have never paid attention too, like the clothes you were wearing, the weather, the furniture. See it all, focusing on every detail and pausing to look at the smallest of details. Write this process down, like a movie script, capturing the entire event from start to finish.
- Once you have imagined the above, replace the limiting belief phrase with the new empowering belief phrase that you created above. Change how the script plays out so that the characters react in a way that makes this new phrase realistic. Do not change the entire scene, but manipulate the dialogue and the reactions of the characters remembering to keep the colours and the scenery the same. Write out this new script.
- Using the power of imagination and visualisation, return to the old memory, once again viewing it from a third person point of view.

Only this time, see the event happening using the new script, ensuring that all characters are following it. You are the director at this point, so make sure everyone is doing their part. Once you are able to see this happening without having to cut and reshoot the scene, and everyone is playing their part perfectly, you can move to the next part — the premiere of your movie.

- Immerse yourself in your new movie, your new memory. Play it in your mind, as if you are there, no longer hovering over like a movie camera, but seeing it with your own eyes at that moment in the past. Remember how it happened, remember this as what *actually* happened. Practice this, and once or twice daily, replay this memory in your mind. Allow it to be the truth, because, after all, it is the truth and soon you will realise that maybe this was the actual memory all along!

Move your body: This is the finishing touch to the masterpiece that you have been painting, and just like Picasso, your work is only finished once you sign your name with a few final strokes of your brush. Your signature completes the work and allows you to move on to other projects. This part is that final stroke, that final signature that completes your reprogramming and locks in the memory as fact, as truth. The mind-body will be aligned, in sync, and propelling you toward your dream life.

- In the beginning, you will most likely have to consciously set out time during your day to focus on this process, finding a quiet place so that you have no interruptions and the least amount of distractions. It takes some effort, but eventually, you will engage in these techniques throughout the day and even while you are actively engaged in other activities. That's when you become a master and no longer need to make special time for this, you'll do it on the fly! You will also be able to do it when your body is at a peak positive state, like exercising or playing Frisbee, and the mind-body connection will be so effective that others will feel your presence and conviction. In the meantime, I want you to stand in front of your bathroom mirror, and remember your new belief nodding your head in agreement and holding your hands to your heart as you say it out loud.

For example: *I remember (nodding your head) when I was in high school and this poor kid who had one pair of shoes, and who's dad picked him up in a beater, suddenly came to school in all the best clothes. He even started to smile more and be less nerdy. I asked him one time what happened, and he said that his family made it big, and he told me that when you have a good idea you can do anything. I remember feeling his emotion. I remember how I knew I could do the same (hold your hands to your heart and feel the truth, feel the memory).*

Stand up tall and make sure you nod your head in agreement and hold those hands to your heart while you go through the new memory in your mind. Do it with your eyes open and make sure you feel it!

Let's recap the process of removing limiting beliefs, reprogramming them, and ensuring they are aligned with the entire mind-body that is you!

Identify the source
Eliminate distortion
Uncover needs
Create alternative aligned beliefs
Create the memory
Move your body

This process can be used to replace memories, but it can also be used to plant new memories, which in turn result in powerful mind-body beliefs that drive the path of your life. You can easily choose a set of beliefs that you would like to have and make them a part of your mind-body. It's like opening up a catalogue, selecting what type of life you want, then picking from a list of thoughts and beliefs that would get you that type of life. Then, you would simply become that type of person — memories and all — inevitably leading you down the path to your desired outcome.

PRINCIPLE 8

SYNCHRONICITY —SOULPLAY

As I stepped outside into the cold crisp air of a typical Canadian winter, I couldn't help but notice how quiet the city was. It was early on a Wednesday morning in November, still too early for morning commuters, and the city had a wonderful quietness to it, as if it was paused in time and I was the only one alive. It made me stop and look up at the office towers, which stood in the distance like sleeping giants, slowly letting out clouds of steam from their rooftops as if they were gently breathing. I took a deep breath of the cold winter air into my lungs and as I exhaled saw my own warm breath gently leaving my mouth and disappearing into the night sky. A wonderful peace and calmness came over me as I stood there on my back deck, now gazing at the stars twinkling directly above me, lost in the moment without a thought or care in the world.

It was easy to be in this state, in just a few hours I would be leaving for Costa Rica and returning to a magical place that we discovered on our previous visit. It was a beautiful morning, and as quickly as I had lost myself, I was pulled back to the present and the time. It was 4:11 am.

I loaded up the suitcases in the back of the truck, and found myself going from calm to excited, being less aware of my surroundings and much more involved on what needed to get done. I closed the trunk and smacked my hands together, rubbing them to create some heat from the friction but mostly because of the overwhelming energy of anticipation that ran through my body. I couldn't wait to get there! In the distance I heard my wife's voice call out, "do we have time for a coffee?" As I darted up the walk, skipping a step to get to the deck and into the house, I responded, "We sure do!"

We made our way to the airport and arrived at the parking lot that sits across the main highway, one kilometre from the airport departures gate. We drove in and began following the posted signs to the area that was currently being filled. The sign said, 'ROW 4', and shortly after we turned into the row we found a spot. The lot was lit up by massive overhead light posts, as the light of day was yet to make an appearance, and in the distance, I could see the exhaust of the blue bus picking up passengers a few rows down. We gathered our things from the console, made sure we had what we needed, and got out of the truck to grab our suitcases. As I pulled out the final bag, I glanced up and realised that the bus was already just a few feet away. The bus had a number on the front, one of those white cardboard square inserts with black numbers that the driver places in the plastic envelope attached to his windshield. It was clearly visible — bus number 11.

I stood there, dazed for a moment, as I realised the connection between the row, the bus number, and the time on my watch from earlier that morning — 4 and 11, 411! I smiled to myself and loaded the suitcases onto the bus. Carla sat down just before me and she could see a strange grin on my face as I sat down next to her. "What's that cheeky grin for?" she asked. I chuckled at her, leaned in and said, "It's cause I'm just so happy we are going to our magical place!" Then I kissed her on the cheek and sat back in my seat.

As we made our way to the airport I began thinking about other times I have had these types of moments, these types of coincidences, and how I had now become very aware of their occurrences. In the past, I was unmoved by such events and easily would have missed this particular synchronicity, yet I still allowed myself to think that I was probably looking into it a little too deeply.

I turned to Carla and we began fantasizing about what we would do when we arrived, and how exciting it was going to be to see the friends we made on our last visit. We were both drenched in excitement and overcome with happiness. We pulled up to the departures level and by now I was lost in my own imagination, thinking about how the journey would unfold and what adventures we would encounter.

Security was pretty normal, hundreds of people herded into a funnel to make their way through a zigzag of fences in a quiet and orderly fashion, always makes me think of sheep following one another on a farm to be wooled. "Don't forget to remove your belts and shoes. Laptops out of your bags on their own tray", is what we heard as we approach the x-ray machine. Carla handed me my boarding pass as she is the one who always takes care of the admin side of our trips, only because she knows I would have probably already left it in the washroom, or thrown it away with my gum wrapper. Needless to say, she knows my wandering mind well.

We pass through security and collect our belongings on the other side. I fumble around trying to put my belt and watch on at the same time so as to be as quick as possible and not hold up the other passengers, but instead I drop my passport, which Carla had handed to me only for the few seconds of passing through the scanner, and in doing so the boarding pass that was within its pages flies out and slowly floats through the air; like a falling leaf swinging back and forth gracefully yet unpredictable in its path. I now have a belt that is on, but undone, a passport on the ground, untied shoes, and a boarding pass disappearing out of reach under the security desk. As I crouch down to intercept the floating pass, with one hand on my belt and one arm at full stretch under the security desk like a drunk stumbling to grab a quarter of the floor, I finally notice for the first time the incredible details listed on the boarding pass. Flight number 411, Seat D row 11. Now I'm not sure if you are following but at this point but I am literally and figuratively floored! I raise my arm up with the boarding pass in my hand and yell out as if I was at a bingo hall and just hit the jackpot, "411, I'm on flight 411!" An incredible electrical sensation pierced my head and travelled throughout my body to every extremity, leaving my toes and fingers tingling with a million needle pricks. In fact, I got a little bit dizzy and the security lady leaned over to ask if I was ok. It took me a moment to realise that I had lost time and essentially fainted for a second or two, and the lady who had been watching me stumble and fumble around was aware enough to notice and crouch down to help me back up. I stood up and, still a little disorientated, saw Carla coming over from the bench where she had calmly been sitting and putting on her shoes. "Flight 411 babe! Seat D...A, B, C, D... the fourth letter! Can you believe it!?" She smiled, assuming that I must have been 'noticing' yet another event, and was quick to lead me away from security and out into the departures shopping corridor to stop me from making even more of a scene.

I began going over it in my head, and realised that no matter how wonderful and accepting Carla was being, she had no knowledge of the prior incidents and most likely thought I was a complete lunatic. But she knew who I was, and allowed me the space to enjoy my wonderful coincidences without judging me too much. I began telling her the events that occurred from the moment I experienced the peace and calmness early that morning to checking the time, noticing the bus, and now this. Yet, as I explained this amazing moment to her, I could feel the magic of it start to dissipate and almost lose the connection and power it moved me with just moments ago. It was as if trying to explain it made it sound too 'normal', and I found myself playing it down the more I spoke about it. She did her best to see the unlikelihood of such events as she always does when I tell her, and she has even become more aware of these types of events herself, yet I still felt that I was losing its electrical charge.

This feeling had occurred many times before. I have always struggled with the automatic dumbing-down that occurs almost immediately after you verbalise an event. It's as if telling someone makes it less real, or better yet, re-focusing on the accepted reality makes it seem less important. I began contemplating this thought and realised how most times this type of synchronistic event is so personal that the proof of its grandeur remains locked in your own subjective mind. How could you ever explain the wonder to someone else unless they accompany each incident with the same awareness and attention? It is so personal, and maybe that's what makes it so beautiful and powerful. It is happening FOR YOU. I also had another thought as we now walked toward our gate, that if I had shared the initial sequence with another person, then they too would be able to witness any more events that might follow. The conundrum, however, is that these events do not advertise, and they are not waiting for the right moment so that you may share it with others.

We sat down at the gate and, as I held the boarding pass in my hand, I explained the sequence of events to Carla once again, this time with every detail that I could possibly recall, hoping that at some point, at some time, she would be with me when the magic unfolded right before both our eyes. We sat and discussed probabilities and how she too was noticing more things happen that seemed unlikely. It was important for me that she understood that if she was aware that they would present themselves, and she too would feel a greater connection to the universe, to god, to life, and then not think that I'm slowly losing my marbles!

We landed in Costa Rica at 11 pm and, like the previous visit, had already booked a hotel for the night so that we didn't have to drive the two-hour journey to our destination of Manuel Antonio immediately after a long day of travel and airports. We did, however, have to find our way from the rental car pick-up area to the hotel somewhere west of the airport in the city of San Jose — which is always an adventure as we never opt for the GPS option on the car. Why would we get GPS when we can experience the exhilaration of being lost in an unknown city, relying on our intuition and the grace of whomever we might encounter to get us to our hotel? The Aloft Hotel, we were told, is about 20-minute drive so we figured we could easily find it if we just followed our roadmap and sought out the main roads clearly named on the map. As per our last visit, the 20-minute journey took us about 45 minutes, taking lefts that felt right, and taking rights because they were the only ones left! We finally arrived and checked into the hotel. The hotel was beautifully modern and contemporary with blue and green neon light tubes jetting along the walls throughout the lobby area. The bar area was vibrant with a few groups of young people sitting in black and white tufted booths along a sunken area directly opposite the check-in counter, and others at chromed stools with red tops perched directly at the bar top. In the distance, a restaurant, now mostly empty, had glass walls allowing you to see the deep blue glow of the swimming pool outside in the hotel courtyard. We loved it and, as we approached the counter, we were greeted warmly and genuinely as is always the case with the amazing people of Costa Rica. We had made it!

The receptionist asked for our passports and, after explaining the amenities of the hotel and the opening hours for the complimentary breakfast, handed us a small envelope that contained our two card keys and directed us to the elevator. We were both now crashing from the high of travel and anticipation, and we didn't really pay full attention to the information that she gave us. We gathered our bags and walked over to the elevators, both smiling from ear to ear, ready to have an amazing sleep and awaken to the next phase of our adventure. Inside the elevator, we realised that we hadn't caught the floor and room number. As I stood waiting for Carla to open the small white envelope, I got a sudden tingle on the back of my neck and the hairs on my arms began to rise with electricity as if I had come into contact with one of those Tesla balls. The charge gained strength, and in the few milliseconds it took for me to lean over and witness Carla open the envelope, my whole body had become a vat of heat and electricity. I could feel the sweat beads on my forehead, and although the humidity levels were super high, the elevator was air conditioned and the beads were definitely a result of the yet unspoken and unconfirmed event to follow. I knew at that precise moment, without even looking, what room number we were in. It was room 411.

That trip to Costa Rica become a turning point in my life. The two weeks were a delicious buffet of magical events that baffled common sense and destroyed any remaining doubt that I might have had about our connection to the architecture of the universe. It opened my heart and soul to the wonders that lay before us, connecting me to 'it' in a way that cannot be explained with simple human language but instead a richer, deeper type of communication that one feels deep down within the soul. This connection was not only my own. Carla too was finding her own connection for the first time; the events were also there for her, and she too was moved!

"You are not a drop in the ocean. You are the entire ocean in a drop." —Rumi

This particular wave of events is one I like to share when introducing the topic of synchronicity. It allows me to feel out where a person is in relation to their own 'connection' to life by listening to their view and opinions of the experiences I just described. The beauty of this particular sequence is that it is number based, which makes it particularly easy to follow and dissect for further analysis if required. This is actually the simplest form of synchronicity, and is the doorway to a more profound and powerful experience that involves much more than numbers and events. I will use this factual event to reinforce your beliefs so that you may experience greater play, or I will destroy the limiting belief that makes you want to believe in coincidences through probabilistic means. Either way, by the end of this section you will be able to tap into this non-causal energy that guides you throughout your life.

Synchronicity, a term first introduced by the psychologist Carl Jung, explains the concept that events are 'meaningful coincidences' if they occur with no causal relationship but yet are seemingly related. It is an event or events that are observed to occur without any form of instigation by any known force, and exceed the accepted forms of probable coincidences. It is not in line with the scientifically approved manner in which our universe operates — known as the Axiom of Causality or Law of Universal Causation, which defines every event as having been caused by a previous event and so on. It is why the 'every action has an equal and opposite reaction' and 'where nothing takes place without a cause' concepts were created and programmed into our mind. Although these concepts and laws explain much of the material world, they cannot explain the magnificent displays of synchronicity that are experienced and documented by so many. At this point, some of you may be thinking that these synchronistic events can be defined as just 'coincidences', and that is perfectly normal because of the previous programming that you were exposed to throughout your life. However, let's just look at what the word 'coincidence' means so that you can differentiate the two and allow your mind to absorb this new way of thinking. Coincidence is defined as the concurrences of events that have no apparent relationship. The key word here is 'apparent'. It immediately insinuates that there *is* a causal relationship, but it's just not visible or 'apparent'. It blankets all events and presupposes that there must be a cause, creating acceptance in your thought process and releasing you of further investigation. Synchronicity has no causal relationship, and when you learn to separate coincidence from powerful synchronicities than you will open the gate to a powerful communication system that has always been there in plain sight but hidden from your understanding. This is Soulplay, and you will use it to guide you through life, to become so connected, so intuitive, that it will change the course of your life.

I have discovered that there are two main benefits or reasons for Soulplay, and although you may find different views and opinions, it is these two that I have embraced because they have continually and consistently guided me to a deep connection with life, making it more magical than I could have ever imagined. It is this magic that has brought me here, and it is this that I share with you. Remember that my relationship with synchronicity may not become yours, and it will be for you to develop your own way of interpreting such magical moments. My purpose for writing these words is so that you may discover the beauty and mystery and allow it to support you in creating a truly blessed life, with everything that you have ever wanted, never afraid, insecure, or hurt but instead always knowing that you have all the answers within and feeling unstoppable in achieving your dreams!

Before I begin, it is important that you understand that in order to enjoy Soulplay, you must first learn how to *be in the now* and allow yourself the opportunity to capture these moments when they occur. There is a time for thinking, for visualizing, for planning, and there is also a time for BEING. It is a time to stop and smell the roses, as they say, and take in all that is happening without past or future thoughts. This is not a meditation or a planned visualisation session, it is a conscious creation to turn your attention to the present and just be in the moment. It's taking a deep breath and focusing on the sounds, the sights, the smells, and then searching out more sounds, sights, and smells happening at that precise moment that you may have not been attentive to a few seconds prior. Being means a heightened sense of awareness for what is happening at that precise moment — the naked and raw present.

Taking the time to just *be* will sharpen your awareness and improve your ability to 'catch' things that occur around you that most people are completely unaware of. You will begin to notice that you are the only one that mentions a certain sound or something happening that the people around you haven't noticed, making you realise that you are beginning to become aware of so much more than before. This skill alone has given me greater intuition about potential dangers, and my friends sometimes call me a wizard for anticipating such events. It is this heightened awareness for the 'now' moments that gives me the opportunity to experience Soulplay on a regular basis.

Another important point to understand is that Soulplay will never present itself to you if you are actively seeking it. You cannot consciously create these moments of connection with the universe, and trying to do so is like trying to watch a bird fly whilst you physically hold it in your hand. You must let it go to witness its flight, and so too is the way of Soulplay. You must release your conscious mind from the equation and be in the now moment. Imagine trying to listen to your favourite radio station without being tuned to the right frequency. No matter how hard you try to hear that station, you never will. The station is still there, it is broadcasting, you just have to find the right channel. Tuning into the Soulplay frequency becomes easy when you learn to enjoy being in the moment.

The first main benefit of Soulplay is KNOWING. Knowing that a powerful connection exists between you and everything around you, knowing that there is so much more to you than the identity you and others have conceptualised, knowing that you are more than an accidental evolutionary hiccup — that you are already everything that you need to be, knowing that your soul is on fire and that you are more powerful and capable than you have ever imagined. This in itself will open the gates to unbounded potential and possibility, instilling inside you a wonderful and magical calmness, a confidence, and a sense of worth that can never be removed by any external means.

The experience of Soulplay is not something you hear about in mainstream media and remains hidden from most people due to its unquantifiable existence. It does not fit in with the current model of beliefs and is therefore tucked away into the shelves of mysticism, only to be found by those who dare seek it. There is no scientific proof that it exists because science itself is pigeonholed into its own dogmas and beliefs, which are completely the opposite to the idea of Soulplay. Once you discover it, the institutional beliefs that you held so high will begin to crumble and you will be freed of the ties that bind you to the current system You will be above the system, using your knowledge to effect it and mould it to your desires. You are beyond the rules and programming they have instilled in your mind and have now discovered a greater force.

There is, however, a small band of researchers and brilliant minds that are finding ways to quantify Soulplay and bring it to the masses. Just like Carl Jung, there is a new movement that is compiling evidence so that those who hold science to be the ultimate truth, can be shown that there is so much more to discover if we just change the parameters that prevent us from doing so. But, my aim is not to give you the evidence and build a case, I will leave that to those whose purpose it has become. Instead, I am here to show you that if you dare, you can experience it for yourself and then all resistance will fade, and you will become a 'knower,' changing how you look at the world forever!

The second benefit of Soulplay is its ability to guide you toward the very thing that you are seeking. Not in the sense that it shows you what to do, but in that it confirms the path that you are on by presenting itself to you. You will see it, and at that instant, you will know that it is there to confirm that the path you are on is the one you are meant to be on. At a time when you are unsure about what your path is, it is your intuition about what the Soulplay event means that will allow you to uncover the right path to take. You will simply acknowledge it and you will know why it occurred and what you should do. Think of it as road signs along a highway, letting you know that an exit is coming, whether you take that exit depends on your assessment of the Soulplay that has occurred. You may have not previously known in your heart if you were going to take the next exit, but after Soulplay, you become connected and your decision was instantly available to you through your intuition.

When you begin to experience Soulplay in this manner, you will find that you are no longer blindsided by events in your life, but instead, you are completely in tune and almost expectant of the things to come. It is this amazing feature that we have been blessed with that makes us so incredibly powerful once we learn to decipher it. This ability or skill will bring an unprecedented amount of wellbeing into your life and to those around you. This is the language of the gods, the link to the universe, the knowing that destroys ego and awakens the soul within making you a true master of destiny.

So, the question that you may be pondering at this time may sound something like this: "how I differentiate Soulplay from just a normal coincidence?"

The answer is simple — you just know!

There will be no doubt in your mind, or more accurately, in your soul that the events are not random and that you have tuned into something that is beyond rational expression, beyond the scientific explanation of probabilities. For those of you that need a more concrete measure than you can use exactly that, the law of probability. Soulplay events are beyond the natural laws of probability, and beyond the laws of cause and effect. They are not tangible, and they are unpredictable beyond any type of scientific inquiry. You must release your dogmas about long-held rational explanations, as the very nature of these events are beyond laws, beyond rules, and can only be interpreted through a higher level of connection. I implore you to expand your awareness and explore the beauty and magic that is Soulplay so that you may realise the incredible power that you already hold.

Master Training

1. Learn to enjoy NOW moments in your life without judgement. Practice being aware of the present by focusing only on the sensory experience that you are receiving at that precise moment in time. Notice the sounds, the smells, the sights, the touch, and most importantly your own presence and involvement in it.

2. Wonder what it means! When you experience an event ask yourself, in wonder, what it could possibly mean and then release it. By asking yourself the question you are invoking your intuition, however, the secret here is to immediately stop analysing the event and return to the moment. Smile and continue being lost in your now moment. It is here that the meaning will be revealed. It is in the act of releasing that the answers will appear, as if they just popped into your mind out of thin air. Trust it and allow it to happen.

3. Enjoy it! Know that you are tapping into the fabric of the universe, the ebb and flow of all things, and that you are finally remembering how to communicate in your true original, but forgotten, language. The language of the universe. The language of your soul.

PRINCIPLE 9

EATING CARROTS, GRATITUDE & THE POWER OF NOW

How many times have you heard the popular saying 'dangling a carrot on a stick', or some form of the same phrase, which directly implies the receiving of a reward or prize somewhere in the future, but only once the current goal or target is achieved? I'm willing to guess that the majority of people reading this have at one time or another heard the phrase and have had a 'carrot' dangled or have dangled such a carrot in front of another fellow human. This popular saying is so entwined in our culture that it is the most used form of motivating people in this capitalistic model of the world we live in.

Now the carrot takes on many forms — money, gifts, promotions, titles, corner offices, trips, emotions, and the list can go on and on until we have exhausted the entire scope of anything that any person may desire and believes they are otherwise unable to obtain. In essence, the entire system we live in is dependent on the idea that any type of success or fulfillment lies in the achievement of a set of goals or accomplishments in the future — 'if you do this, you will get that.' The key is understanding that this statement is telling you that fulfillment is not here and now, but somewhere in the future.

Now, before I explain why this concept is the reason why so many people suffer from an ever-growing range of mental and spiritual conditions, I want to tell you that by knowing how you were fooled into its machine-like grip you will be able to regain the ability to completely transform your life experience and find real fulfillment. Even more so, you will be able to see how the grim prospect of death is not only absurd, but fantastically man-made through a carefully crafted system of beliefs that keep you from discovering your true power. We will destroy these beliefs so that you may look upon the world in a manner that excites, fulfills, and nourishes your whole being.

As you discovered in the Power of GIVE, it is important to have goals, steps, and something to work toward to satisfy those ultimate feelings that we crave. We need to have those carrots available for us to eat in the future, however, it is here that the problem arises creating a mental plague that is causing human beings to ignore their soul needs and focus on their physical needs alone. This dis-balance or dis-ease results in what can be described as the sensation of something missing in life, and eventually to what we refer to as bad mental health. This is the single biggest issue facing mankind today, yet we do not teach our children to understand this because most of the adult world doesn't know. This principle alone will change how you feel about your life, even if all else remains the same.

'Carroting' is how we will refer to the anticipation of eventually arriving at a future reward from this point forward and, just like all future rewards, it is in the anticipation of the 'feeling' that we will potentially experience from that reward that drives our motivation. Just like the story of the young boy who, while sitting on a cart, dangled a carrot on a stick in front of his mule. The mule walked toward the carrot, which always remained just ever so slightly out of reach, pulling the cart and the boy forward toward his destination. The illusion of attainability moves the donkey in whatever direction the boy decides, never questioning his master's path. We can hope that when the boy arrives at his destination he allows his donkey to eat the carrot, satisfying our humanity in knowing that the poor donkey didn't make an ass out of himself for nothing.

The problem with human carrots, and carroting, is that we have been conditioned from a very young age to want more and more carrots. In fact, it is the pursuit of carrots and not their consumption that we have been programmed to want. We identify our existence by chasing and anticipating carrots, yet we never get the feeling and enjoyment of eating them because we must at once chase the next carrot. The socio-economic system we live in can only work with humans chasing carrots that promise feelings of fulfillment, yet ensure that you are too preoccupied with the next, even more enticing, largest of carrots, that you completely ignore the present carrot you hold in your hand — never satisfying your fulfillment needs that were initially anticipated. The whole being is unaligned and unbalanced, quickly seeking physical pleasures via destructive means.

I want to explain to you how and why understanding this principle — as opposed to just telling you to practice gratitude and listing a set of ways to do it like most books and self-help guides advise — will give you the ability to truly comprehend its effectiveness and use the power of NOW, and gratitude, to redefine you as a human being and open a passage to a purpose-filled, exciting, and satisfying life. Just following a list is like giving a poor man a fish, *knowing* the origins and understanding its effectiveness is teaching the man to build a boat to catch his own fish! I want you to catch your own fish, and never be fooled by the illusion of 'carroting' again.

This programming starts at birth, and by the time you get to kindergarten you are already learning the very basic concept of anticipation, learning that there are more grades ahead and the climbing of the proverbial ladder begins with the preparation for grade school. Then you move on to grade one, and begin anticipating the next grade, and then the next. By grade six, the education system, along with every adult in your life, has reinforced the belief that you must carry on up the ladder of school so that one day you can become somebody. In fact, by this point the idea of having fun, being overly creative, or even preoccupied with the beauty of the present moment, has been replaced by seriousness, conformity, and the expectation of how you should behave, and how that behaviour will define who you become. A set of values is being instilled in you, such as money, education, status, and power are the ultimate definition of 'being somebody'— the 'carroting' has begun!

Junior high brings feelings of insecurity and doubt, perhaps you begin to get anxious about whether or not you can actually be the somebody you're expected to be. You find ways to fit in and be part of the 'cool' groups because, from your point of view, they seem like they will definitely be somebody. You find a job so that you can earn some money to buy the latest jeans so that maybe, just maybe, you'll be part of the 'in crowd' and you too will feel like you are, and will be, somebody. The individualistic, ego-based identity begins to form, and you unwittingly find yourself fitting in somewhere that you believe you identify with.

High school arrives, and every adult you know who has already passed through the system preaches their wisdom to you as if their lives were so much better, or could have been better if they had focused on their grades, made more money, had more status, and been somebody. Exams take on greater meaning, and the anticipation, the carrot, of becoming somebody is always there, always dangling, always bigger than before. You climb the ladder of high school and reach grade 12, and although it should feel great to be a senior, it lasts for about five minutes because now you have to think about college or university and the next step. Your world is surrounded by expectation and the 'carroting' never subsides, yet you can see that if you keep going forward, keep climbing the ladder, eventually you will be somebody. You now understand that this is the way, so you get good grades and you go to university.

University is amazing! There are professors, and degrees, and fraternities, and all the while you find yourself feeling like there's something more for you. That feeling drives your persona and you join other students in a specialised area that promises to deliver that feeling of significance and purpose that you have been working toward since birth, since kindergarten. You are so close, and you can see how this career will give you money and the ability to have great things and eventually be somebody. The pace is relentless, and you are surrounded by like-minded people, all looking to be somebody. Every person, every aspect of the environment is perfectly created to ensure that you continue to pursue or, more accurately, continue chasing the carrot to ultimate life satisfaction.

You are now part of the machine, and will eventually become a co-conspirator in driving this machine forward. Like you, the professors once came through the system and now are cogs in a machine they will claim is the highest form of human achievement, never eluding to the fact that the truest and highest form of human achievement is living life on your terms, unless of course they have discovered this and have passed on a tidbit of 'enlightening' wisdom about the reality of what is to come.

You are now ready to go out into the real world and be a somebody — to finally find those wonderful feelings associated with making it! Finally grabbing that damn elusive fucking carrot!

You find yourself a great job in a great firm and you feel pretty good, however, you begin realizing that there are only a few positions at the very top within the firm, and in order to get there you must dominate, grind, and hustle. You learn to be ruthless and ambitious, treating those with less education or drive as inferior and easily dismissed, and those with similar traits as you, as the competition. You are hungry, and the carrot is so big and juicy now that you can almost taste it. You give up sleep, time, and you spend money on material things so that you can be seen as belonging to the right 'in' group and although you feel anxious deep down inside — like something is not quite right — you dismiss it because you still hold onto the comfort of almost being there, almost being somebody!

And then one day it happens! You are the president of the firm and, as you sit in your corner office contemplating your life, you think to yourself that surely this must be it, this must be what I was waiting for! You begin to wonder if this is the 'somebody' you were supposed to be, and you decide that this must be it. You have arrived. Except there's a problem. It doesn't feel like you thought it would and you don't feel very fulfilled at all. In fact, this carrot tastes like all the other fucking carrots!

Then you come to the conclusion that this isn't it. There is another bigger and better carrot and it must be when you take over the entire company. So, at 60, you find yourself chasing more carrots until the final days when you look back and wish you had smelt the roses, enjoyed eating each and every damn carrot, and took the time to do the things that felt great.

I hope you can see now that if you allow yourself to continue carroting, not only will you find yourself unfulfilled, but you will also realise how much of an ass you were — someone that followed the carrot in whatever direction it took you, never once forging your own path, or stopping to smell the wonderful flowers that lay so close on the path next to you. During that journey, you sacrificed your life experience for that ultimate carrot and now have no way of ever getting it back.

The heaviness of regret can weigh down on a human when they see the drawing of the final curtain. There can only exist sadness when the end arrives, and the disconnection of your mind-body and soul makes death a scary place, a place of regret and sadness instead of another adventure. Learning to use gratitude will allow you to appreciate and absorb the ecstasy of fulfillment throughout your life, no matter its length. Reprogramming this belief and consciously being grateful for the simplest of things brings wonder and magic to the present and changes your perception of life, allowing you to experience a timeless life. You can die an old man or woman never having really lived, but you can also die today and feel like you have lived a lifetime. This shift begins with gratitude, and choosing to find those things that are wonderful, as opposed to seeking out in default fashion all the negative things that you experience. You get to choose what you focus on, and if you have followed along from the start then you already have all the tools you need to be in the right mind and to use your new skills to seek out the positive and focus on the opportunity. Understanding the power of gratitude and using it in conjunction with all that you have learnt thus far, and adding the next component to your arsenal — the power of 'now' will bring massive change to your life.

So far, we have discussed many concepts, and some have required a deeper level of thinking than just day-to-day thoughts. I have asked you to be aware, and contemplate many areas of your life, so that you may understand yourself as a whole being. After you have mastered these concepts and processes, you will be able to effectively manage yourself almost automatically and subconsciously. At this point in your learning, I am going to ask you to release all those things we have discussed throughout this book so that you may actively engage in the present moment. Just like we did in Soulplay, it is in the NOW moments that we practice our gratitude. And just like in the time loop method where you learnt in the power of GIVE, you will also learn to be grateful for things that have occurred in the past, or are yet to occur, but always doing so in the present moment. Gratitude in the present moment means that you are able to appreciate the wonderful things that are currently in your present awareness, and you are never consumed by the anticipation of things to come. You will never wish away days because of a future event you are looking forward to. You will never use phrases like 'I wish it was the weekend' or 'I can't wait till summer' or 'When I get that promotion I will be happier.' these phrases are so common today, and they are part of the lack of fulfillment in most people's lives. These sentences are defining your life experience and programming your subconscious by stealing the enjoyment of life right from under your nose. If you can't enjoy the present you will never be able to enjoy the future, because when the future arrives, it will be the present, and you don't know how to enjoy the present!

Being here, now, means taking the time to enjoy the present regardless of what you have planned in the future, or what has happened in the past. By being in the moment and seeking out all the great things right here, right now, you will begin to shift your feelings and your life experience. Every day that you are alive has many things to enjoy and be grateful for. There is never *nothing* to be grateful for (unless you are determined to believe that there isn't) — the ability to take a deep breath, or feel the sun on your face, is such a gift in itself! Believe me when I tell you that even if you manage to achieve all your goals, you will still find yourself feeling unfulfilled at the end of your life if you don't practice being grateful in your present. If you can't appreciate where you are now, you will never appreciate where you are in the future!

Gratitude in-the-now means that you savour that damn carrot every time you hold it, and when the next carrot is attained it too tastes just as sweet. This simple reprogramming in your perception will create a momentum in your life, unlike anything you have ever experienced before. Unlike the donkey who passed his favourite flowers that he normally loves to eat because he was so determined to get the carrot, you now have the ability to train your mind to notice and feast on the wonders around you right now. You will enjoy all the present wonders and also enjoy the carrot when it becomes present. This will destroy the programmed 'carroting' lie that has been instilled in you since birth, and give you back the beauty of your life experience regardless of the circumstances.

As I mentioned previously, you can also use the present moment to be grateful for past and future events making you a master of gratitude. This can also help with altering any negative feelings associated with previous events and fears of future feelings of potential events. By being grateful for events in the past you can rewire your past experiences, creating a past that is aligned with what you desire. By consciously choosing events that have scarred or affected you in the past, you change your mindset from victimisation to empowerment and will no longer identify with those negative feelings. The subconscious does not know the difference between a real memory and an implanted one. Knowing this, we can add great feelings and gratitude to past events that might otherwise seem bleak and traumatizing. You do this by changing your focus to the things that you could have been grateful for and being grateful in the now!

In the Power of GIVE you learned how to visualise like a master, using techniques that very few people have ever heard about. The time loop method allows you to go back in time and see an event from a third person perspective, implanting a new memory, but it also allows you to be grateful for the things that you had never paid attention to before because of the emotional charge of the negative event. See yourself, and be grateful for what you went through and how it has led you to a better path today. There is always something to be grateful for. Remember to always make a positive gratitude not a 'could have been worse' viewpoint. The trick is to find five small things, that in hindsight, were pretty great. The clothes you had on, your friends and family, the experience to grow, the intuition you already had that was awakening — be there in the now, and be grateful. This should also be done for past achievements, and positive times where you failed to be grateful but now realise you should have been. Go back and relive it, being as grateful as if you were there at this moment.

There are cultures that have the process and power of gratitude engrained in their belief systems from an early age, and this type of programming results in a completely different life experience for their people as a whole — especially when it comes to death. When you appreciate the now and are grateful for the wonders happening around you, you do not have the capacity to fear the proverbial end. Once you realise that the 'carroting' scam that you have been programmed with is what actually created your fear, only then will you begin to find relief from the existential crisis. When you are always anticipating and searching for the next carrot, hoping that it will fulfill you, then death can only mean that you will never be fulfilled. It is the greatest trick the devil has played on your mind. Even if you lived for 200 years, you would still need more time because 'carroting' is the unattainable future. Today is the tomorrow you were dreaming about yesterday! Gratitude, here and now, is freedom!

<u>Master Training</u>

5 Amazing Things!

Get yourself a diary and title it '5 Amazing Things.' Each night write down five things that you are grateful for. This is a 10-minute exercise, not something to ponder for too long. Simply go back to the start of your day and find five things that are pretty damn amazing. They could be anything from, 'I had an amazing extra-long hot shower this morning that felt great' to 'I got home, and my partner had made me my favorite dinner'. Scan your day from start to finish with your only focus being to find positive things that you are grateful for. You will notice that it may seem like a chore at first, but once you get going you could probably list at least 10 things. If you have a partner, and would like to release the day's stress together, sit together taking turns, without judgement and without expectations, revealing the things you are grateful for.

NOW carrot!

Eat your carrots! Use a bracelet or ring that is associated with gratitude (available in the Soul on Fire box) so that you are reminded throughout the day to be grateful in the NOW. Whenever something makes you smile or feel good, look at your bracelet, touch it, and pledge your gratitude. It can be as simple as, "I love how my co-worker made me smile just now. I'm so grateful!"

Morning carrot!

Set yourself up for an amazing day by reading your steps and proclaiming your intention for the day. My favourite place is right in front of the mirror, before I brush my teeth, or in the shower while the water trickles over my head. I like to say the following:

"I am so grateful to have this new day. I will make it the best day possible, and choose to see all the amazing things it holds. I will be awesome today. Thank you for this new day!"

You can use that intention, or put your own spin on it. Just remember to *feel* the gratitude of having another day to live — eat that damn carrot.

Night time carrot!

The last thing you should do before you go to sleep is to put yourself in the right state of mind for rest and intuitive dreams. When you're finally laying down for the night, release all your plans and thoughts for tomorrow. They will be there waiting, so there is no need to think about them. Instead, close your eyes and take deep breathes, being grateful for the opportunity to rest and recharge. All the answers that you need will come to you if you just let things go. Take this time to congratulate yourself for being on this path to a greater and better you, and thank the universe for the insights and awareness that you are being blessed with.

PRINCIPLE 10

INTUITION —THE LANGUAGE OF THE GODS

Most people believe that language is one of the greatest achievements of the human race, and the biggest differentiator of intelligence amongst the animal kingdom. Through the use of language, we can proclaim in hundreds of different ways that we are the most intelligent beings on the earth today. Of course, this very proclamation should immediately make you question the validity of that statement. Yes, the truth is that thinking we are the most intelligent proves that we are not. In fact, we truly have no way of knowing if we are the most intelligent, as it is we alone that create the system and tools to measure intelligence. How we can we be so arrogant to assume that our method of measuring intelligence is the *right* method.

I'm going to take this a little bit further, and into a territory that you may have never had to tread on until this particular point in your life. You probably agree with the statement I made about human intelligence perhaps being the least intelligent due to its inability to understand the 'larger' picture of life. This is because you have previously been exposed to the idea of keeping an open mind about things and have also probably learnt values that conflict with bold and arrogant statements of superiority. 'Hitler' and 'white supremacy' are written words that immediately bring up programmed feelings and beliefs, making it easier for you to agree with the statement regarding the belief about human intelligence and more importantly the lack of it. Even if you do think that my statement is false, you are easily swayed to the possibility that the statement is true and perhaps, in fact, we are the least intelligent.

However, this next one goes against all the programming you have been exposed too throughout your life, against all of your preprogrammed ideals and beliefs, and against the greatest threat and hurdle of all — dogma. Spoken language did not make humans better at communicating, it actually imposed very strict rules with preconceived meanings that dictate the desired and prescribed reality. Language is the 'dumbing down' of humanity and the reason for the lost ability to communicate through other means. In 'abracadabra' you learned how powerful words can be and how our society is shaped and moulded by them. Each culture has their own version of a state-educated communication system that is devoid of the truest form of connection and communication that we possess as powerful whole beings — intuition!

Intuition is just a small part of the ancient, non-verbal language that we as whole beings where capable of having with each other before we were boxed into a system of predesigned grammatical languages. Perhaps you can imagine it as a feeling, a knowing, a way of communicating that transcends vocalisation. The best way I can describe it to you is perhaps as a sort of telepathy, for lack of a better word. Once the soul took on its body or vessel, it was taught to speak the verbal language so as to keep its power and ability hidden. This hidden secret power allowed you to not only communicate with others but also be completely connected to the universe itself, sharing in her intimate knowledge of all things and always in perfect sync. In fact, the universe and all her wonderful permutations have been trying to communicate with you since day one, sending out her signals like a radio station sends out their broadcast over the airwaves — except there are no listeners. No one is tuned into the right frequency! The messages are there for you, you just have to look for the right station and tune in!

This lost language is the bridge between the physical world and the spiritual world, and although the haze and fog of distractions may prevent you from crossing, it is still there, eternally constructed with fabric from the heavens. It is the place where your soul once resided, and where it instinctively knew how to speak the language of the gods. The ability to communicate in this manner is still there deep within you, deep inside your being, it is your soul, it is god! Reconnecting with your soul and strengthening your intuitive nature will give you the ability to remember this power and begin using it as a whole being, reminding you of your true essence and power.

In Soulplay you discovered that you are connected to the universe, that you are a part of it and not just an outside observer. You learned how this form of communication is happening with you and not to you, and you also discovered how this dance between you and the universe may be able to guide you through your human experience, helping you when you need it most. It is there to awaken your connection to the hidden form of communication we call intuition. This intuition can only be cultivated and strengthened once you have opened your awareness to the beauty of Soulplay, and in doing so, you will begin to 'remember' or more accurately you will discover a feeling of 'knowing' of what it is actually saying to you. The point I'm trying to make here is that Intuition is a part of Soulplay, and without tuning into the frequency, without the awareness of Soulplay, you will never be able to decipher what is being said.

The hardest part of understanding the language of the gods is not in deciphering it, because it doesn't have form or function as a normal human language would have. In fact, it has no rhyme or reason and follows no grammatical boundaries. It is boundless 'knowingness' and does not adhere to time and space as we comprehend them. The very definition of intuition refers to its Immediacy in communicating its desired meaning without any rational or logical interference. You know *NOW*, and you understand it deep within your soul. It is much more than a 'gut' feeling because such feelings can be physical in nature caused by anxiety or expectations, and although they are powerful tools in themselves, they are influenced by the ego and can lead you down the wrong path. With intuition, there is no delay and no thought distortion.

I want to share with you the intuitive nature of my life, however, as you may already know, this knowledge and connection is something that happens for you, and you alone! Once you try and explain it in common human language it immediately loses its lustre and potency. It's like trying to tell someone a story that, in your mind, is fantastically amazing, yet once you get halfway you realise that your words have not only lost the audience, but you too now realise how unimportant it sounds. It's usually followed by a 'you had to be there,' which in turn makes you question the grandness of it all.

When this intuitiveness begins to awaken within you, it does so within your own subjective experience and very rarely is it shareable with others. In fact, it begins to sound pretty damn crazy when you verbalise it and bring it into the real world. It does, however, on very rare occasions encompass not just your subjective experience, but also those around you. Let me tell you about a personal experience that may resonate with you, and allow you to understand that this knowledge is not something you can explain to those who do not know. Even now, I can give you the tools to discover it, but I can't really 'show' you how powerful of a force it is in my life, I can only tell the story and hope that a little bit of its magic comes through. Even then, the point is not for me to convince you of how connected I feel, because only I will ever understand that — the point is for you to discover it for yourself.

About a year ago my wife and I were in Phoenix, Arizona on our usual getaway from the cold reality of a long Canadian winter, and although we had been there many times before this particular trip stood out in my mind. The reason it stood out is because I had a very unique intuitive experience that was also experienced by four other people around me, something that is very rare and extremely impressive when it occurs. It was a truly remarkable connection that happened without any attempt on my part to make it so, but instead, a pure intuitive experience that left everyone mesmerised by its awesomeness.

Our Phoenix trips were always about escape. Escaping from the cold, the stress of our hectic lives, and the opportunity to turn off our phones and computers and just enjoy a quick four-day break to recharge the soul. It usually consisted of many hours spent by the pool reading our favorite books, sipping on cocktails and taking in the sunshine, followed by a couple of nights out on the town. One of those was a night at the casino. Now before you make assumptions, let me clarify that we went for the live music, the entertainment that comes with meeting random strangers at the centre bar, and a very controlled $100 per person limit on the roulette table. Neither of us are big gamblers, as we both understand that the house is designed to be the winner, so we accepted the potential loss of our $200 total as part of the entertainment fee that we were willing to pay to the aforementioned 'house'.

Our casino night was always a great time, and we've met some pretty amazing people during our bi-yearly visits to the centre bar. Believe me, it was worth the $200 to just be able to sit and speak with a smorgasbord of fascinating personalities that could only be found in an Arizona casino at midnight. We would always begin with a cocktail and some casual conversation with the barkeep, followed by the live music of the resident band playing at the stage next to us, which immediately drew in a few hundred people, and then more cocktails and conversation but this time with whatever characters had moved in next to us at the bar.

There was always a great vibe that surrounded the bar as most people in this area were not consumed with the gaming part of the casino, but instead more inclined to drink, dance, and engage with other fellow humans. It was for this reason that we loved coming to the casino and to this bar in particular. Had it not been for the live music and the varied guests, we would of probably have never made the effort to visit the casino, and would have had $200 in our pocket, as the roulette portion of the evening would not be enough to convince us to visit. Nevertheless, this combination of activities made for a fun-filled, air-conditioned night that satisfied our needs after a long day in the sun.

The day the incident occurred, I had already been experiencing a heightened sense of awareness for a few days prior, which had put me in an amazing balanced state where I felt relaxed, connected, and in perfect sync with who I was and how my life was playing out. I had truly discovered that I had no fear in life and was enjoying every moment of it. Everything happened as it should, and my energy and vibration were super high — I felt fearless. Not an egotistical and imposing type of fearlessness, and not a swashbuckling attitude of disregard for things, but a profound connection to the universe that made me feel like I was in the embrace of my mother's arms at all times. This is how I have learned to live my life, and you can too if you follow the principles and open your heart to the possibilities.

This manner of living led me to the casino on this particular trip and directly to the centre bar for our usual pre-live music cocktails. It was unusually quiet, with only a handful of people sitting at the counter and the majority fixated on a gaming machine sunk into the bar every few seats. The sounds of the casino were louder than usual, and I couldn't decide if it was my heightened sense of awareness that had my ears well-tuned, or if it was just the lack of chatter that usually seemed so abundant when we arrived. I immediately asked the bartender why it was so quiet, and he confirmed my suspicion — there would be no live music that evening. Any other time we would have left to find a live music venue, but we had arranged to meet another couple who we had met on a previous visit, so we opted to stay and wait. While we waited for our friends, we ordered a cocktail and met the bartender that was serving our section of the centre bar. He was a young man, with brown short spiky hair, no older than 28 or 29, and we spent some time talking about the decision by the casino to no longer have live music on Friday nights in November. While we were talking, I noticed that I was sitting in front of one of the in-counter gaming machines, and grabbed a $20 bill and inserted it into the flashing slit that seems to demand your money. I don't know why I played, as I had never in the past fed the bar machine, but on this occasion, an impulse told me to do it, so I did.

My wife looked at me surprised and asked, "You're going to play that?" As the machine grabbed and pulled my 20-dollar bill into its belly, I turned to her and said, "Yeah, let's try it together while we wait!" As she moved closer, she brought her glass toward me for a cheers and we heard the bartender as he moved on to other waiting customers say, "Good luck!" We sipped our drinks and chose the poker game, which was the only one I was remotely familiar with, and hit the GO button without much thought or attention to what the hell we were actually betting. When we hit the button the second time, the machine began flashing its light, and I quickly realised that we had just got a hand that won. We both looked at each other, smiled and giggled, and then watched as the machine credits continued to climb one by one — 21,22,23,24,25... 100, 101,102. It wasn't stopping! Now we were laughing, mouths open in surprise, as we watched the credits continue to increase as the machine 'dinged' its digital bell — a sound that must be magical and addictive to those that play obsessively. The machine finally stopped at $500! A $20 bill turned to $500 on the first round and only the second touch of a button!

The bartender came over and congratulated us on the big win. He couldn't believe that we had gotten so lucky so quickly! We looked at each other, smiled, and clinked our glasses together once again as I quickly hit the payout button and ensure we collected our $500 prize. This visit was to be paid for by the casino, and I was so grateful for having been given this wonderful gift that I would not allow greed to disconnect me from the beauty of my very intuitive state that I had been in all week. It was this blissful relinquishment of control and hyper-awareness that was causing everything to play out perfectly for me. Everything around me was happening with such great detail, and even though we had just won a nice chunk of change, I was so immersed into every sound, every image, and every scent that my wife said I almost brushed it off as quickly as I won it! We sat there with smiles on our faces and enjoyed meaningful conversation about our goals and dreams and as we always do, laughed about how we had become so connected to each other and to our wonderful life together. We always had a way of imagining our futures without ever losing touch with the beauty of what was already happening in our present moment, and it was this ability that allowed us truly to enjoy our lives. We had come a long way, and we had created a way of being together that strengthened our dreams and brought them into our reality without struggle or grind, we had total belief in everything that we wanted because we already had it all. Our life was this — grateful and immersed in the now, yet always building to the next adventure.

Half an hour passed quickly, and our friends arrived at the bar with the usual banter of excited greetings and hugs that have become synonymous with our way of being. We shared the usual complimentary conversation, followed by the update on the lack of live music, and the decision to stay for a drink and play it by ear. They sat down with us at the bar and we began sharing stories and catching up on each other's lives since the last time we met up a year ago. It was a yearly catch-up, yet their energy and spirit created a seamless connection as if we had just seen each other last week. We enjoyed the company, and were happy to have met people that were positive and likeminded, always leading to good laughs and positive conversation.

I glanced toward the bartender and he immediately caught my eye and came over to take a drink order. As he did, I couldn't help but notice how I was super aware of all the things happening around me. It was as if I was experiencing everything in slow motion, and every moment of sensory input was detailed beyond description. I could hear the words from various conversations happening in the distance and at the same time be completely in tune with the discussions within our own group. I was noticing how many people were wearing hats, how many had red dresses or shirts on, the shoes that people were wearing, the scent of cigars from the high limit room in the distance, as well as the wonderfully spicy perfume on the lady who had just walked past in a black dress. It was almost surreal — I felt so in tune and so awake. As the bartender approached, I noticed that they were showing the Formula One time trials on the TV screens in the background, and in particular, at that precise second, I noticed a time stamp on the top corner of the screen that read '10:05'.

Now, before I tell you what happened I need to clarify a few things so that you can understand how powerful intuition truly is and how inconceivable it can appear to those that are not in tune. The first thing is that the time-lag between me seeing the time stamp of 10:05 and the thought and words I spoke directly after was less than a second, and at no time did I consciously think about what I perceived and what I suddenly 'knew' and verbalised. In fact, there were no CTPs or STPs (Conscious Thought Patterns or Subconscious Thought Patterns) happening at any point during this intuitive experience. It is this that makes it so raw and so powerful, and it is this that defines a perfect intuitive experience.

Secondly, I will never be able to explain in human language what this feeling of 'knowing' is, because it is not language or thought, it is beyond our recognisable language and hence why I have called it the language of the gods. Once again, all I can do is attempt to put into words something that is not explainable in words, so that you may get a glimpse of what it could be like once you tune in and discover it for yourself. In order for you to be able to speak this language, you will need to understand that you can't rationalise your way into learning it. You already are fluent in it, you just have to trust that it is there, and that you will know it when it happens.

Now, back to my story. Just as I noticed the timestamp of 10:05, I turned to the bartender who was now standing directly in front of me and I said, "You were born on October 5!" The bartender's brow wrinkled, his eyes squinted, and a look of curiosity and confusion consumed his face. "How do you know that?" he asked with a strange grin now starting to develop. Carla and our friends had also just heard what I had uttered, and they too were now totally focused on what had just happened. The bartender continued to look at me and grin, waiting for me to relieve him of his agonising curiosity, so without too much thought, I said, "I just knew." The bartender, who had been leaning toward me over the counter with both arms extended out in front of him, now stepped back into the bar area and smiled as if he knew what had just happened and he said, "That's a good trick, how did you do that?" Just as he asked, questions began to pop up from the other people around me. "Ok Ricardo, how the hell did you know that?" asked one of them, followed by a comment from Carla as she giggled, "He just does that sometimes!"

Now, I want to explain that at this point I am still very aware of everything that is happening, and I am totally sure that If I explain to them what I had just experienced they will think that I am bat-shit crazy, or more likely they will all already be pre-disposed to believe that it's a trick and I must have figured it out in some sort of logical manner. The truth is that no matter what I say, there is no one except me that understands how powerful and immediate this communication can be. I knew at that moment that this was a real and authentic intuitive experience, and so I laughed and responded, "It's just a little mind control trick I learned, but I can't tell you how I do it, that would take away the mystery!" And the truth is, I don't know how I do it! I just know that if I allow myself to be in the right state of mind, I can tap into it and realise that I am connected to everything.

The next 20 minutes consisted of the bartender trying to coerce the secret on how I managed to know his birthday from me. Imagine if I told him that I saw it on the TV screen and just figured it out. He would still refuse to believe me, and demand a reasonable and 'logical' explanation. One that I just didn't have! I knew what I said at that moment was true, and there was no wavering or thinking, it was pure faith in the message that I received, and no scientific experiment can be conducted to prove it.

Master Training

I want you to think about a time in your life when you may have had an intuitive experience and then I want you to ask yourself the following questions that confirm if it truly was a genuine occurrence or just a gut feeling. Take a moment to go back through your life and pick out those moments that you may have dismissed as a fluke. Return to that time with this new knowledge and understanding of intuition. These questions are designed to filter out the 'gut feeling' types of experiences, which are not intuitive (although they are still valuable). True intuitive experiences are not distorted by any kind of thinking, they just are!

1. Was the 'knowing' immediate?

2. Did you feel like it was 'strange' or 'weird'?

3. Were you 100% sure of the outcome?

These three simple questions will allow you to not only identify intuitive experiences, but also create a platform from which you can understand them when they arise in the future. Once you acknowledge that you have had a genuine experience, you will begin to understand what it is like to be fearless. When you connect and communicate with the universe, you will begin to understand that you are more than you ever imagined, and life will begin to unfold in a way that you never thought possible.

You already know how to communicate in 'The Language of the Gods' for it was the first language you spoke and the 'knowing' is already within you. The secret is to not try and experience it, but instead to create the right conditions for it to occur for you naturally. In 'abracadabra' you learned how words are essentially spells and can create the 'reality' of your physical life, now with 'The Language of the Gods' you can also stay in touch with your spiritual reality. Using the physical language along with the language of the gods will enable you to live this life here on earth in a way that fulfills and enriches you. These, along with the teachings in the other principles, are part of your preparation to living your greatest life!

PRINCIPLE 11

FAITH — YOU MUST BELIEVE IT TO SEE IT!

I, like most people, used to live my life with the belief that if I can't see something with my own two eyes, if I can't experience whatever it is you're talking about with my own real and true physical senses, then it's probably not true. I can think of countless times throughout my life when someone told me about something they experienced that was outside of my understanding and I would immediately question the validity of their experience based solely on my limited beliefs. "I have to see it myself," was a common statement, and was an accepted form of challenge since science and scientism was the all-powerful decider of questionable occurrences. And it wasn't just me, this was the defining principle of the reality we lived in, and any argument could be pulverised into non-existence by the mere sound of the word 'science'.

The irony in all of this is that most of the 'laws' of science are also based on presumptions made by a few people that the majority now assume as reality. The truth is that even the most solid 'laws' of science are still based on a 'theoretical' mathematical equations plugged with numbers made of symbols that have been fixed to make it all work out according to the currently held belief. Even right now your idea of what a nebula, or atom, looks like is a construct of data that has been carefully crafted into an image that suits your eyes. In fact, none of those images are 'real' images and have been sold to you in a manner that makes you think that you are actually seeing something that only exists on a graph. They understand that if they show you, if your eyes see it, then you will believe it!

I am not trying to diminish the importance or validity of science, but what I am trying to do is to open your mind to the power of the physical senses when it comes to belief, and how they can be manipulated into complete conformity when you are not aligned with the non-physical part of your being. When you have learned and can understand the previous 10 principles, you can easily comprehend how this occurs and how the majority of people are imprisoned by these beliefs. Knowing that there is more to the game than meets the eye will give you the ability to choose what you want to believe, but more importantly, it will awaken in you the power of faith which delivers to you, and to all, anything and everything that you have ever truly wanted. It is here that I will show you how everything that you have learned thus far can be used to create a way of being that will bring you a lifetime of health, happiness, and wealth.

At this point I also need you to understand that the 'faith' that I am discussing with you here is not the faith that man-made religions of the world have placed upon its followers. This type of religious faith does require belief without physical confirmation and, although it is similar, it differs in the sense that although you have to believe it first, with religious faith you potentially may never see it! You may have to have faith in a god that you never actually see or hear, and may only meet when you have expired on this earth and pass on to the other side. Religious faith rarely shows its face in this beautiful journey we call life and instead hides behind the veil of death. The faith I am talking about here is one that will appear to you in this lifetime and in this reality, it will let you see it in all its splendour and give to you everything that you have ever wanted!

At this time I want to clarify that I am not arguing against, or in favor, of any religion or faith — on the contrary, there is beauty and value in many facets of religion and to discuss those here would lead us off course. What I can tell you, and what you already have learned thus far, is that the foundation of all religion is based on programmed beliefs and that your religious inclination, whether it is abstract or based on strict adherence, is *learned*. The principles you are being taught here are in harmony with any and all religious beliefs as we are not attempting to define a god, but instead, develop a way that allows you to maintain whichever religious beliefs you choose and weave them into this powerful new way of being. A way that allows you to be one with the entire fabric of the universe, discovering the ability to witness your own creations, your own dreams, coming to full fruition in this reality and in this lifetime.

When you have fully grasped the other principles within this book, you will be ready to use this 'faith' that I'm presenting here to you today. With this you will become a true master of your own destiny, freeing you from the clutches of fear and lack, giving you a wonderful internal peace, an eternal knowing and a life that is fulfilling and rich in every way. This ability is already within you and has been from the beginning, but you were never taught that it was there, and you were definitely not given the tools to even tap into it. It has been presented before in many forms and in various language terms such as 'prayer' and 'law of attraction', however, without the foundational knowledge that you have been learning within these pages, those methods would have no real effect on your life. You now have the missing ingredients that you needed to allow 'faith' to begin presenting you with real-life occurrences of magic and wonder, unlike anything you have ever experienced before.

You may be wondering this — how do I create things and experiences into my life using faith?

The answer is made up of two parts that together will unlock your ability. First, you must learn and practice the other principles within this book and be a raw and naked whole being, fully aware of who and what you truly are. This part is necessary, and if you skipped to this last principle without immersing yourself in the other principles first, then you may miss the mark and never awaken the power that lies dormant within you at this very moment. Leave your baggage, your ego, and your limiting beliefs at the door and go down the rabbit hole, follow the principles, and then you can join us here at the second part, or second step, to creating your life using faith.

The second part to unlocking this power is 'knowing'. Yes, we have already discussed this word in previous principles but now we will apply it to the power of faith. Just as in Soulplay, where you realised that there really is a connection between what you perceive as the 'external' world and your own 'being', this part uses that same connection, that same knowing that you are not separate from the universe but in fact an active participant in everything and everyone. This creates within you the right kind of faith, a faith that believes in something first and then sees it come into reality. It is the unwavering knowledge that something will occur with absolute certitude, not only in your mind (both conscious and subconscious) but also deep down in your heart — in your soul.

This type of certitude can only be felt with an absolute belief and can be difficult to experience at first due to anyone, or more, currently held limiting beliefs that may prevent it from being. I can explain this to you by giving you an example of something that you have a complete and absolute certainty about at this moment, and extrapolate the type of certitude that you will require in order to use this last principle. It also means that if you practice the other principles, you can learn to program your mind to eventually have the right thinking and the right soul connection to create your own life by design, becoming a fearless whole being.

Now I want you to imagine for a minute that you are standing on top of a common, regular sized, dining chair. As you look down toward the floor you are able to consciously assume that there is a two foot, maybe a foot-and-a-half, distance between your feet standing on the chair and the floor beneath. Now, I want you to imagine jumping off that chair and notice that your mind will create an image in your head, that is practically automatic, of you landing on the floor. Sounds like a no-brainer, but let's probe a little deeper. If you can once again imagine yourself standing on the chair but this time I don't want you to jump, instead I want you to ask yourself this simple question: "What will happen when I jump off this chair?" You probably already noticed that the moment you ask the question, your mind automatically knows the outcome. It doesn't even need to give you the image first, it already assumes the answer. There are no details required to assess the situation. You know with certitude that you will land on the floor. There are no limiting beliefs, no resistance, no doubt about it, correct? This is the type of faith, the type of certitude required to make this last principle the greatest power you possess.

So the question is not what *type* of faith it is, because you can clearly see and understand it by this simple story, instead, the question is: *how do I have that type of faith when it comes to creating the life I desire?* Most manifestation guides or books will tell you to use emotion and feel as if the desired outcome was already present. Although this is part of it, without knowing with absolute certitude, your feelings will only be contradicting the desired result because they may still hold resistance that is subconsciously ingrained. It is this that most people struggle with when it comes to creating and manifesting the greatest life possible. In order to see the life you want, you have to believe with absolute certainty that it is inevitable — just like landing on the floor when you jump off a chair, your desired outcome must feel like an inevitability.

So, to answer the question, all we need to do is simply learn the 10 previous principles, but especially the principle of Soulplay! Once you reach a point of awareness that allows you to experience Soulplay on a regular basis, then you can begin to use this final principle to its fullest potential. By witnessing the miracle of connectedness in your life, and realising that you are one with the entire universe, then the type of faith required will begin to grow inside of you. You will understand that you are already creating life, and have been from the beginning. When you know deep within your heart that you are part of something bigger then you could have possibly imagined, you will 'know' that you can truly have everything that you have ever wanted. This knowing, this faith, this certitude, is the missing ingredient that can only be cultivated through awareness and experience. Now you have all the tools!

Master Training

Think about a time in your life when you were completely certain about something and then it came to be. Use a positive experience. Example: I knew that I would find a way to afford that trip and I did! OR I knew deep inside that I would get that job!

1. Write down the thoughts you had when you realised that the outcome was certain.

2. Did you worry or have doubts that it would happen as you pictured?

3. How did it make you feel when you were right about your faith in the outcome?

Notice how there is never any doubt or worry when you have complete faith in a specific outcome. It never crosses your mind, so the outcome has to be in-line with your faith. The feelings you get once your faith is validated are the feelings that you can use to strengthen your ability to be in this state for all the things you desire.

Language patterns to use:

- Like the sun rises daily in the east, so will the _____(desired outcome)
- I know that the sun shines bright just as I know that_____(desired outcome)
- Witnessing this moment of Soulplay proves that I am connected, and I am creating!
- I know my life is a direct reflection of the quality of my thoughts, and the depth of connection to my soul.
- I am grateful for being connected, for being aware, for being a creator.

Remember that nothing in life happens to you, it only happens for you!

THE FINAL WORD

You may have struggled with believing in such a power when you first began reading this book, but now you know that this is not only just a possibility, it is the greatest form of living that a whole human being can experience. These principles will awaken you to the powerful creative force that you are, and will give you the strength and wisdom to live your greatest life.

Once you have stripped down the conditioning, torn off the masks and costumes, you reclaim your true self and become aligned with your authentic nature. After you have shed this excess baggage and reconnected with the soul, you discover that life begins to meld to your every desire and you awaken... to become a Raw, Naked, and Fearless whole being!

ACKNOWLEDGEMENTS

Everyone I have ever met, from the day I was conceived to this very moment, has had a part to play in the writing of this Manifesto. This book would not exist as it does if I had never met that teacher, or ignored that phone call, or turned left that day instead of right. So many things happened precisely and inevitably that allowed this particular book to be written, and this particular journey of mine to arrive at this junction here today. Even 'you', by reading this book, have become a part of my story and, although we may have never met, you too are now another ripple in the pond that is my life. In fact, we have always been connected and by reading this book you will finally remember that you are just as important to me as I am to you. So first and foremost, I thank you for your involvement in the making of this book, and for allowing me to be a ripple in your pond!

I would like to thank my best friend and the defender of my soul, my wife, Carla Dreger for not only allowing me to pursue my purpose, but to actively encourage me at every junction. She was there when I was lost, guiding me as best she could. A beacon of light when life was dark, always believing in me, in us, until the only possible outcome was a beautiful life together. Thank you, my love, for teaching me, for listening to me, and for loving me!

Maria Leal and Avelino Leal are the two greatest human beings I have ever met. Sure, you can call me biased based on the small insignificant fact that they are my parents, but the truth is that they really are unlike most parents and have accidentally revealed their superpowers to me on various occasions throughout my life. I suspected that they were extraterrestrial beings from a young age and as I reached my teens I began to understand that they only tried to keep it hidden so as to protect me from my own inherited yet dormant powers. My parents are not the greatest HUMAN beings... they are SUPERHUMAN beings and I love them with all my soul! Their values and morals were passed on to me and I chose to keep them. With them, and because of them, I have written this book.

My brother and lifelong friend Carlos Soares, who always told me that I was destined for greatness, even when I didn't see it, always saw something in me and always encouraged me to find it. I'm sure he thought I would or could be an astrophysicist, but instead, I chose a very different path and one which for the first time really does feel like greatness. Thank you, my friend and brother, for always believing in me, and for being brave enough to listen to my teachings and coming along for the ride.

I would also like to thank my editor/proof-reader/book consultant/critic etcetera, Lindsay Shapka, who I happened to find through a recommendation by someone who I had never met that had responded to my LinkedIn post. Our professional relationship was built on an assortment of random online events that led me to her and to our initial email conversation; and although she may not know it, our meeting was and always had been the only possible connection that could have ever led to making this book happen. Thank you.

ABOUT THE AUTHOR

Ricardo Cruz Leal is a certified clinical hypnotherapist and life success coach who helps people with finding their authentic selves to live a healthy happy and abundant life.

Learn more about Ricardo and how he can help you live your best life at ricardocruzleal.com.

Made in the USA
San Bernardino, CA
15 August 2018